ELEVATE WITHOUT A

Mate

Winning While Single in Christ

Copyright © 2020

WRITTEN BY: VASHA TOLBERT

Table of Contents

ELEVATE WITHOUT A

Mate

Winning While Single in Christ

Prologue

*"Success isn't about how much money you make.
It's about the difference you make in people's
lives." – Michelle Obama*

"Hello, Ms. Tolbert, this is the gynecologist office. You were here for your Pap smear a few weeks ago and we have received your test results. Unfortunately, your Pap test was abnormal. According to the results, you have an incurable disease and we will need to schedule a follow-up appointment to re-test you." These were the words of defeat I heard over the phone while sitting on the edge of my bed. Not only was I undergoing an unwanted pregnancy, but now adding to my sorrow was the news of an incurable disease. My life was crumbling, and I was not equipped to put the pieces back together; honestly, I wasn't even sure if I wanted to. I felt defeated like all hope was lost. My dreams and goals rapidly scurried out the window. My gut tossed and turned, and I was infuriated. How could I have been so stupid? How could I have had sex aimlessly without considering the potential repercussions? What was I thinking? I encountered a whole new level of defeat, one that completely imprisoned and held me captive. The stench of defeat left a residue of a polluted odor and an overbearing feeling of scornful hopelessness in my heart and mind. The very thought of failure caused my heart to sink into my chest. It was like being anchored to a metal wrecking ball and dropped in the middle of the ocean. There was only one direction to go from this point: further down. This was the lowest and darkest time of my life and all I wanted to do was dig myself out of this gaping hole that had swallowed me. My life was spiraling out of control. I was at a place where rock bottom cradled me, and grief became my daily companion. Defeat was what I deserved for being so careless, so, defeat is what I received, so I thought. I had nothing to give or offer to anyone. How could I ever win with a loss like this? "Ms.

Tolbert, Ms. Tolbert", the nurse continued. "Are you still there?" With a deflated voice, I responded, "Yes, I am here" – wherever "here" is.

I was failing miserably. I'd been bothered by the fact that success had now seemed impossible. I struggled for years with digging myself out of this hole. I was single and lost.

Who do I look to? Where do I go? For the longest time, I overlooked the advantages of singleness and spent a great deal of time complaining about it. I didn't feel it was worth celebrating, but I knew that for me to enjoy all the good that life had for me, a change would be required. I would have to change my life and my perspective. In my times of despair, God has been ever-present. But I still had questions. Why was I still single? What was the purpose of abstaining? Was it not good for me to be alone? I found myself existing solely for my future, so I failed to live in my present. It was easier to live in my future because that's the place where all my wishes, hopes and dreams would be a reality; I detested my present. I despised the beginning of my journey. How much longer would I need to abstain from sex? How much more deprived will I be of companionship and intimacy? Doesn't God know that I want to have sex like everyone else? These were questions that ran through my mind often. How can I win while single? Is it too late to win? What about all the mistakes I've made? Is it possible to elevate without a mate?

Oftentimes when mentoring young adults, I urge abstinence, but are there cons with abstaining? Absolutely, and sexual frustration is one of them. Personally, I am quite moody when sexual frustration takes its toll. And, I believe, it's natural. I'm sure you think that once you convert to becoming a believer, your sexual desires just die at the altar. I confess this is a mythical belief and is not the case for many Christians who desire marriage. Many, like myself, have struggled and continue to struggle with controlling this fire of passion in our pants or under our skirts. I even decided to name this unquenchable and random fire; I call it a flesh flare. It's basically a random desire for physical stimulation. I have experienced random moments where I burn with a want for physical intimacy – it can become overbearing. And at first, I didn't know how to deal with these sporadic flares. Who do you talk to about this? How do you counteract your desire to engage in sexual activities, when you shouldn't? I know what it feels like to want to give up on yourself and allow the temptation to take over and you often feel as though you are at your wit's end. But, keep going. Keep trying to please God. Keep hoping. Keep praying. Keep seeking Christ. Give every day your best shot. The Holy Spirit knows our innermost thoughts and intents of our hearts. The Bible even tells us that there will be a struggle for most singles, in which I will discourse later. But I want to share some tools with you that have helped me develop in my faith and strengthened me in the process. Has this single and no sex thing been perfect? Absolutely, not! Do I still struggle with a few things? Absolutely, yes! However, I will be as real and transparent with you as possible, so that you too can win while single.

My nine-year journey of no sex has been intriguing to say the least. I have learned that you don't have to wait until you're practically married, to begin enjoying your life. You can start today, and you can start with yourself. You can become an even better version of yourself. Nothing is impossible with God. You can elevate without a mate. Abstinence with Jesus is achievable, and the benefits are rewarding. I have attained nine years of abstinence guided by the Holy Spirit. Have you heard the saying, "God keeps those who want to be kept"? That is partly true, however, I believe, He will even keep us when we don't want to be kept. God has kept me in times when my wish wasn't to be kept. He kept me when I wanted to have sex. His will overpowered my will many times. Even when your body is weak, and the enticement is beyond imagination, God will continue to keep you from impurity. He will make a way for you to escape what seems to be overbearing temptation.

Whenever my mentee asks questions surrounding my God-given ability to abstain, I always respond with a prerequisite; abstaining from sex is a journey. It takes time, patience, discipline, determination, and resilience to go against the grain. The finest things in life endure a process. I equate the process to waking up and pressing forward every day, with the hope that today I'll meet "the one", I can get married and finally receive companionship and intimacy. But with each new day, instead of a spouse, came new faith. God renewed my mind and faith daily. I'll be honest and say that if God had told me in my first year of beginning abstinence that I would be on this journey nine years plus, I would more than likely have opted out. I would have called it quits early on. I would not have selected to become abstinent out of curiosity or self-will. It wasn't something I saw reasonable to do. What was the point? Why abstain? No one else that I knew was doing it. Why start with me? I saw absolutely no point. See, that is the funny thing about God; He leads us on our journey but doesn't always give us the full picture for every page of our story. He only asks that we trust Him throughout our journey.

There have been times along this journey that, out of desperation, I would have settled for anyone. Settling for anyone sounded better than waiting on "the one". Then I'm reminded that God can do exceedingly, abundantly, and above all that we are able to ask or even think (Ephesians 3:20). Don't settle, but secure. He intends for us to prosper and wants to keep us from harm. God wants success for you. He wants you to be successfully single. We can rest assured knowing that we have what it takes to secure the promises of God. We weren't created to settle, but to secure everything that rightly belongs to us. I have learned through the process of elevation that faith presents durability. To be quite honest, it is challenging to endure trials, uncertainty, isolation, indifference, hardship, and adversity.

Did you know the societal acceptance of singles is much more acceptable today than before? As of 2016, the U.S. Census Bureau reported that there are 106 million unmarried people residing in America from the age of 18 and older (https://www.census.gov/newsroom/facts-forfeatures/2017/single-americans-week.html).

The standardized family structure of what a household resembled in the 1900s has drastically changed in comparison to today's household. The dichotomy of today's family structure could range anywhere from two families living under one roof varying from four young adult roommates saving on housing expenses while putting themselves through college. The make-up of a household is more unorthodox than ever. A large part of these changes is influenced by economics, culture, social status, and individual goals. Knowing this poses a question for me, how can singles survive the struggles of carrying economic burdens, strive to pursue oneness with Christ, and not compromise their integrity to get ahead? It is possible. God wants more than anything to give us the knowledge and tools we need to win. The word of God lets us know that wisdom is the principal thing; therefore, get wisdom: and with all our getting of wisdom, get understanding (Proverbs 4:7). Together, we will gain insight and foresight along with understanding God's will for singles and the power of singleness. God wants to unlock your next level and He wants to give you the keys that will defeat every barrier prohibiting you from becoming the woman or man He predestined. You can elevate without a mate. You can start winning in Christ while you are single. Are you ready to begin?

If you've ever visited a church or gone to Sunday School, I'm sure you're familiar with the story of Adam and Eve. Did you know that Adam unlocked the key tools to winning without Eve? Adam proved his leadership and prestige ability to dominate without a mate; he elevated without a mate. What does one do until that special one arrives? How best can you prepare mentally, physically, spiritually, and organically? How can you overcome the struggles that cause discouragement? Is there grace for your gift?

Your time and effort spent while single is essential. This time is needed to cultivate your core skills and lead in your role as a single. Use this time to prepare for greatness, prepare for elevation, do the work, and prepare some more… and then, apply the things you have been preparing. In other words, occupy, occupy, and occupy. The First Lady of my church has a key philosophical dialog which is, *occupy until Jesus comes,* and I agree with her. Singles have undivided time to prepare, build, and lead, so, do everything God gives you to do. A great place to start is with the vision God has given you. Build the life you want to lead. If you don't love where you are now, that's okay – start building the life you love. You can begin today. Start with an idea or vision, set a deadline, and step out on faith. Mental, physical, spiritual, and organic preparation is essential in gaining a good grasp towards lasting achievement. Not only do we want to accomplish a successful season of singleness, but we want longevity in success. We need to be mentally equipped to handle the strains of success. We need to be spiritually grounded to execute our God-given purpose. We want to be organic and authentic in our season of singleness. We want our relationship with Jesus to be organic and strengthened. Why is this important? Because, there will be struggles with doing anything successfully, and this includes being single. Discouragement will try to invite itself into your life, but, know that God has grace for the gift of singleness.

One of the first things I had to let go of was the art of comparison. When the love of Christ invades our lives, our own plans and our own will must evade or leave. To evade something simply means to avoid it. I challenge you to avoid your own depiction of success. If we want to see absolute success, our plans must evade as Christ invades. As Christ enters, what we had in mind for our lives must exit. Although you may have thought that you'd be married by the age of thirty with three beautiful, bright children, God's purpose may not mirror what you had in mind but it doesn't mean He is not leading you into elevation where there is purpose, peace, and prosperity. You are valuable, you are loved, and God has a strategically successful plan intended for your life. I think the film *The Help* says it even better – You is kind. You is smart. You is important!

Now I am not an expert in the game of chess, but I do know that chess can be complex and require forward thinking. In this game you must prepare to lose a few game pieces, but the aim of the game is to protect the king. The most strategic players play with the end in mind, so every move is tactful, thoughtful and deliberate. Great chess players understand that the quality of the play achieves the win, not the number of players. With that in mind, please note that your purpose and worth are not found in the number of people who surround you, but in the quality of God within you. Psalms 18:30 (NIV) says, *"As for God, His way is perfect: The Lord's word is flawless; He shields all who take refuge in Him."* The queen in this game is the most diversified and effective player but sometimes a pawn is sacrificed to shield the king. Now, please understand that the key to winning is making sure that your most viable pieces are reserved and not jeopardized. Sometimes, God will reserve and preserve you by hiding you in singleness to keep you from jeopardizing your destiny. You are essential to Him, so He is establishing and molding you into his perfect treasure for His special purpose. In the bible, God illustrated through His servant, Gideon, that He can win challenges and battles. God gained victory through Gideon with the least amount of people. God doesn't elevate according to our numerical value, instead, He elevates according to one's character, courage, faith, and integrity.

Parallel to the game of chess where all pieces protect a king, you and I also have a King to protect. We serve the King of Kings and the Lord of Lords and He reigns in us. It was David that said, and I paraphrase, we are to hide His word in our hearts and protect it, so that we may win and not sin against God, our King (Psalms 119:11). Regardless of our opponents' schemes and conspiracies, we can win while single in Christ. It doesn't matter how many players you are teamed-up with or against, the quality and strategic plan of God will get you to where you need to be. Are you ready to achieve greater?

1. The Art of Comparison

Galatians 6:4 (NIV) "Each one should test their own actions. Then they can take pride in themselves alone, without comparing themselves to someone else."

After finding out about my illness, I didn't know where the heck to start. What was next? I now knew what loosing felt like. If I was going to hope again, I needed a game plan. I needed courage and resilience. I was about a month pregnant at the time. I debated just having an abortion. Who was I kidding? I couldn't raise a kid. It's one thing to lose and it's an even greater challenge to lose with a kid. If I was going to keep the kid, I didn't want the kid to be stuck with a loser parent. That would suck! So, I did what I thought would be best. I started creating one-year goals, five-year goals, etc. I begin setting timelines and creating new things to hope for. I buckled down on my focus. I prayed to God to rid of the disease and I promised Him that I'd keep the kid if He did. I didn't know if He heard me or if He'd even do it. In due course, I scheduled my return visit to the gynecologist to get retested. Nearly a month after retesting, and much prayer, the nurse reported receiving my results back. And before I could even say that I'd rather not know, she went on saying, that I'd tested negative. I was blown away about what God had done for me. If you are where I was, I want you to know there is hope. You can do so much with so little faith.

Amid loosing, I understood watching and competing against others in order to win wouldn't be that helpful. Instead I'd probably be even more miserable. I think comparing ourselves to others robs us of the individuality we offer to the world. I once heard that if you continuously compete with others you become bitter but if you continuously compete with yourself, you become better. It's easy to become a habitual offender in the art of comparison. I know this personally because

I compare myself to others without realizing it. For instance, within a few minutes of downtime spent on my phone I find myself scrolling down my newsfeed comparing my life to the lives of others, and most times I'm not sure how or when I began scrolling and looking at the pictures. But this psychiatric warfare of comparison and the need to know what everyone else was doing in their lives would continue for hours. I would compare their life to mine and judge my life by theirs. Whenever I'd see someone post negative concerns, I would suddenly feel good about myself, thinking, "Hey, at least it's not me." Then, I would continue scrolling. When I found others, whose lives appeared so much better on social media than mine, I would suddenly feel discouraged, thinking to myself "What am I not doing right" or "I should be so much further than where I am". The art of comparison ultimately only led to me feeling empty. When we compare ourselves by ourselves, this is not wise, and we are left at a disadvantage when we do so because, we all didn't start at the same starting line and neither of our races are straight shots to the finish line.

You may possess something that best equips you for your race and someone else may be distinctively gifted for their race, so grow in your God-given grace for your race.

How do we break the art of comparison over our minds? We can begin defeating the art of comparison by not conforming to the commonalities around us, but being transformed by the renewing of our minds, so that we may prove what is that good and acceptable and perfect will of God for our lives. Breaking bad habits and thoughts in our minds can lead to ultimate fulfillment. Comparison is the act or initiation of measuring one thing to another. When we choose to compare, we choose to conform to the trends and upkeep required to keep up with the next person. At the end of the day, pretending to be like someone else is draining.

One of the ways I broke the art of comparison was by verbally complimenting someone else. If I liked what another woman was wearing, instead of comparing myself to her, I'd simply compliment her. Years ago, there was a certain colleague of mine who was absolutely gorgeous and stunning; I mean, she looked like a life-size Barbie doll. She was unique and was her own woman. She owned her style and she was confident. We'll call her Betty. Betty had beautiful long hair that was always neatly brushed. She wore extravagant, full circle dresses, that complimented her stilettos so well. My dresses didn't

complement my purse as well as Betty's stilettos did her dresses. Whenever I passed by her at work, I had two choices; I could choose to compare myself to her and wallow in my apprehensiveness and lack of confidence, or compliment her, so I chose to defeat the art of comparison and give her the compliments she deserved. Betty and I eventually became great acquaintances. Oddly as it may sound, complimenting others makes me feel better about myself; when I give compliments rather than comparing myself, I'm usually complimented in return. Oftentimes I receive compliments on things that are just second nature to me, like my smile and jubilant attitude.

Sometimes you need to just break the ice and sow the seed of inspiration because you never know how you may impact someone else's life. I have gained great relationships by planting seeds of encouragement and in return have found value in the gifts I possess. I challenge you to compliment and not compare and remember that we can do better together than we can apart. We are the light of the world. When will we start shining our light?

Philippians 4:8
"Finally, brethren, whatsoever things are true, whatsoever things are honest, whatsoever things are just, whatsoever things are pure, whatsoever things are lovely, whatsoever things are of good report; if there be any virtue, and if there be any praise, think on these things."

There are so many benefits to being single, and each of us needs to see ourselves as a unique design of our Creator, God. There are over 7 billion people on the planet and each one is distinctively different from the other. No two people are exactly alike. Why is this important to keep in mind as a single person? Proverbs 23:7 (author's version) says, "For as a person thinks of themselves in their heart, so are they to be." We have the ability to think ourselves into our next dimension. We can think ourselves into the highest and best version of us. The world needs what you have to offer, because God didn't give your specific gift to anyone else, so use it for His glory. The power of our thoughts is essential to the remaining aspects of our lives. Everything we speak begins with a thought, so when we think good things, we speak good things. Think on things that add value to you in this season of your life. Avoid pondering things that take away your peace and bring discouragement. Keep in mind that you have an adversary, the devil, who desires to steal your joy, kill your passion, and destroy your identity in Christ, and he does this through your thoughts. Singleness is a gift from God to you. It's a time to learn yourself, to learn about Him, and to grow into who He has called you to be without distractions. I have learned to enjoy my time and the liberty that comes with being single. If I aspire to travel, I can do so without the need to schedule or coordinate around another person's work schedule, such as a spouse. Your priorities are not like that of a married individual, so take advantage of the benefit you have by maintaining a more flexible schedule. There are minor domestic duties tied into singleness. God minimizes your responsibilities to maximize your recognition of His presence, provision, and purpose for your life. It's important to treasure the gift of singleness. You can't maximize a gift you don't manage. Manage the season of singleness and you will be able to maximize so many wonderful advantages you may not have known are accessible. Begin taking inventory of your schedule and how you use your time. Jot down some day-to-day tasks that you'd like to do more of. When we identify the areas that we can maximize a little more, we'll be able to enjoy a lot more of the benefits to being single. Maximizing your schedule and recognition of God's presence and direction is the first step in order to take ownership of your singleness. Take ownership of your time. Take ownership of your destiny. Grab your goals by the rein and charge forward.

What are some things you can do while single that you may not be able to instantaneously do with a mate? Do you enjoy traveling? Where are some places you would enjoy relishing in? What are some things on your bucket list? Are you looking to further your education? What steps are you taking today that will positively impact your future? How soon can you begin putting those plans into motion? When you finally meet the person you are to marry, what will you bring into the relationship financially, spiritually, intellectually, and skillfully?

Because everyone is so distinctively different, we should never compare our paths of life to each other's; and although our intended ends will differ, we should celebrate their uniqueness. For instance, if your desire to be married with three beautiful children does not come to fruition by age 30, but your friend seems to be living your dream, celebrate and compliment their accomplishments. God hasn't forgotten about you; He has a specifically tailored design for your life.

And I mean, think it through, bitterness won't make anything better, so celebrate, compliment, and sow the seed of inspiration. Your time is coming. In order to genuinely compliment someone else, we must first be able to truly think good things about ourselves.

I learned very quickly in high school that the art of comparison could potentially threaten the best of my high school experience. I had three best friends in high school named Breanna, Robin, and Kia. Breanna's skin was so soft; it looked like caramel coated candy. Her parents spoiled her. Breanna was a perky varsity cheerleader. Robin was light-skinned and had legs of a model. She loved to rock her T-Boz haircuts. She had beautiful eyes, coupled with a bright, wide smile. Robin was kindhearted and sweet. Kia was from Connecticut and had recently moved to Florida. Kia was smart. Her skin constantly glowed as though she sunbathed for an essence photoshoot. Her physique was shaped like a coke bottle. And then there was me. My face constantly broke out with acne. I was goofy and careless. My friends had similarities and differences, and I noticed that my upbringing varied quite a bit from all of them.

All three of my best friends were drop dead gorgeous. I'd even say they were some of the most gorgeous girls in our high school. They were beautiful and talented. It amazed me how we became such good friends because we all had very different upbringings and outlooks on life. My father passed away a few years before I began high school, leaving my mother with five children to raise independently. My mother was forced to leave her stay-at-home motherly duties to join the workforce. She started working as a newspaper deliverer in order to make ends meet. The job demanded seven days a week and an after-hour schedule. The hours of operation fell between 2:30 am and potentially 8:00 am. Eventually, at the age of fourteen, I acquired my first job with the same newspaper company obtaining my first paper route. My siblings and I would all wake up at two o'clock in the morning and head to the newspaper company. We'd package and prepare the newspapers for delivery. I drove and tossed newspapers in hundreds of driveways first thing in the morning and every day of the week.

There were times when I would be tardy for school in order to make sure my paper route was completed. Hanging out with my friends and hearing their adolescent and youthful conversations about boyfriends and the latest trends never seemed to pique an interest in me. I was mainly concentrated on making sure that I was helping my family by taking care of household needs and graduating on time. Shortly, I learned that comparing my life, my journey, and my purpose to my friends, just didn't make sense. Our journeys contrasted greatly. My friends weren't bad people because they were different, and just because I had to mature much faster than my companions didn't mean that I was better than them. I simply took the approach of appreciating the differences that others brought to the table. Advantages can be gained through indifferences as well as similarities. Willingly discussing their contrary backgrounds, upbringings, and journeys allowed me to take a step back and escape into someone else's reality through interaction. Celebrating their differences and complimenting them for their uniqueness inspired me.

"Comparison is the death of joy." — Mark Twain

There was a great soldier in the Bible by the name of Gideon; he was strong in appearance, but shallow in faith. In the days of Gideon, Israel was oppressed by the Midianites. Things had gotten so bad that during Israel's harvest Gideon hid his harvest in order to keep the Midianites from taking it. Gideon was living in fear, insomuch that he hid his blessings from his enemies in fear of opposition. In the midst of trouble, Gideon hid. When God told Gideon that He would be the one to save Israel from their enemies, Gideon worried that he didn't have what it took to walk into his purpose. He compared himself to his peers and lineage. He was a warrior that worried whether God would come through for him. Gideon fell into the art of comparison and began comparing his finances; he told God that he was poor and did not have the financial backing needed to deliver Israel. He, overall, saw himself as inadequate and suffered from low self-esteem. Are you a warrior that worries? So was Gideon, but he still gained victory despite his cowering. Despite his intimidation, he elevated. He was presented the ultimatum of hiding or elevating. He had to choose to cower or cultivate. Will you hide or will you partner with heaven? God doesn't bless us to hide; He blesses us for His glory and elevates us so that His heavenly glory can be evident here in the earth. So, if you're going to partner with heaven, you can't hide anymore. Believe God. Trust God. The art of comparison robs us from fulfilling our purpose. For God to do something amazing through you, you must let go of your past mistakes. No more hiding your blessings in fear of the enemy. God didn't call Gideon to be just like his father, instead, He called Gideon to lead Israel into victory. God may be calling you to do something that you are unfamiliar with; He may be calling you to do something He hasn't called anyone else to do - and that's okay.

Whatever He has called you to do, believe that you can do it through Christ. God called Noah to build an ark and save the world, and nowhere else is it recorded in Scripture where God called any other individual to build an ark. God called Adam to be the first human being. Adam didn't have a predecessor; he only had the voice of God. The same applies to Gideon, who did not have a mentor to train him to lead; God didn't send him to a bootcamp to bench press four sets of six reps, however, Gideon already had everything he needed to access his purpose, and so do you. Talk to God about your insecurities, even though He already knows the things we struggle with. Matthew 6:8 says, *"for your Father knows what things you have need of before you ask him."*

Sometimes we get lost, and don't have a clue who we really are. It's easy to get caught up in who everyone else wants you to be. Praying to God truthfully about my self-confidence helped me evolve into His image of me, as opposed to the image

I had of myself. Gideon may not have had the support of his family, but he stepped out on faith anyways. He stopped hiding and partnered with heaven. Are you willing to go forth despite your circumstances? I urge you to step forward without the influence from the cynical, without the financial backing you think necessary, without that mentor, step forward without having all the pieces lined up. Don't be intimidated by your destiny and your calling, and don't compare, compliment instead.

Weaponry of Defenses

"The weapons we fight with are not the weapons of the world.
On the contrary, they have divine power to demolish strongholds." 2 Corinthians10:4 (NIV)

In the movie Home Alone, there was a boy named Kevin

who had a heated argument with his mother the night before the family's vacation departure. Kevin told his mother that he wished his family would disappear. To his surprise, the very next morning, he got his wish – his family disappeared. The family flew to Paris, accidentally leaving little Kevin behind and alone at home. While his family was away on a Christmas vacation, two thieves were plotting to break into Kevin's home. Kevin overheard the thieves discussing the time they anticipated breaking into his house, but instead of running, Kevin chose to prepare a game plan to fight back. Kevin put together a strategy to defeat the thieves by setting up scare tactics and began searching his home for weaponry. He used ornaments, tar, nails, cans of paint and so forth to scare off the thieves. Ultimately, Kevin defeated the two thieves. They were caught and arrested because of Kevin's fearless preparation and game plan. Like Kevin, God has entrusted us with gifts and weaponry as a method of protection. Although the weapons of our warfare are not carnal, but mighty through God to the pulling down of strongholds, when the enemy plots to break in to steal, kill, and destroy the promises of God entrusted to us, we have the power to speak the Word of God. We are equipped to setup our defenses around and inside our earthen vessels; our mind, soul and spirit - to protect it.

I think Kevin's Home Alone experience can teach us a thing or two in our everyday lives. Your mind, soul, and spirit are your home. God tells us in 1 Peter 2:5 (NIV), we are *"like living stones, that are being built into a spiritual house to be a holy priesthood, offering spiritual sacrifices acceptable to God through Jesus Christ."* We too have a home that we are entrusted to protect. And like the good father God is, He has already given us the tools we need to fight back when the enemy attacks. We don't have to run because Jesus has already defeated the devil; now you have the victory. You can choose to be single and winning in Christ, and I truly believe, you can elevate without a mate. Like Kevin with his family, we can become ungrateful and forget all the wonderful things God has begun in us, and what He has done both for us and through us. When you feel the urge to wish you were in a different season of your life, remember that singleness is working for you and not against you. You can simply use the weaponry God has given you by faith and take your joy back. God has armed and equipped every believer with weaponry of defenses. He has given us these tools to defeat anything that exalts itself against His word in our lives. Be encouraged to know that some tools may just need to be recognized, developed, and sharpened, and the good news is, you are well-able to utilize them. There are still tools I am discovering as I grow in my faith in Jesus. The more I put my trust in Him, the more I grasp the opportunity to fine tune these weaponries of defense.

I believe that faith is the most vital tool within our kit of defense. In fact, faith is the one tool that pleases God and without faith, it is impossible to please Him. Faith is the hope that overflows on the inside of you. Faith re-assures you to believe for the best despite your worst. It's your expectation and a sense of confidence that God has already given you the victory before crossing the finish line. I challenge you to finish with faith. Faith can cause you to stand against adversity. We must hold tight to faith when we feel pressed to compare ourselves to others. Faith will lead you in the opposite direction of your feelings. Faith whispers, "you are wonderfully and beautifully made". Faith shouts "you are more than a conqueror". Faith is a gift from God. He gives to every man and woman the measure of faith, and the measurement of faith we start with may not be the same measurement of faith we end with. Did you know that faith has the power to grow? We can recognize, develop, and sharpen our tool of faith daily. God believes in you and is constantly challenging you to grow your faith. Let's commit to elevating our level of faith. When I found out I had an incurable disease I lost all self-confidence and self-love, and to elevate in faith, I had to receive God's love, mercy, and grace towards me, which, in all honesty, I did not deserve. Eventually, I witnessed God's healing power. He totally healed me through my faith. I am no longer bound by an incurable disease and it amazes me, because His grace and mercy are always on standby waiting to be attached to my faith. With God all things are possible. Just believe.

Self-love is placing a high regard on your happiness and welfare. Many singles desire a spouse in order to feel loved, as a matter of fact, we all seek love and desire it in its purest form. To truly be loved by someone is a wonderful thing. As a single, it's frightening to entertain the thought that you may never experience the love shared in a holy union, but I want to challenge you today to understand that there is no love comparable to God's love for you. With or without a mate, no one will be able to love you like God loves you. He is like a father who wants nothing but the absolute best for you. Even when we make mistakes and our humanity is seen more often in us than His divinity, He is gracious enough to forgive us. There is nothing that can keep us from His love. Knowing this alone, can open the door to really loving yourself. Self-love is irreplaceable. What are some things you adore about yourself? What does self-love mean to you? What negative things are you holding onto that you really need to let go of? Have you forgiven yourself for those mistakes? What is your go-to regimen to engage in self-care? How we love ourselves sets the bar on how we expect others to love us. In order to freely and truly love someone else we must be willing to love ourselves. The word of God says that we love God, because He first loved us. God is love, and when He loved us, He opened the door for us to love Him. There are godly and goodly relationships that God will strategically place in your life, that you will not be able to access and attain without first becoming love. We were drawn to Christ by lovingkindness. Love draws love. Allow the love you have for yourself to draw someone else. Martin Luther King, Jr. stated that darkness cannot drive out darkness; only light can do that. Hate cannot drive out hate; only love can do that.

"And Jesus answering saith unto them, Have faith in God. For verily I say unto you, That whosoever shall say unto this mountain, Be thou removed, and be thou cast into the sea; and shall not doubt in his heart, but shall believe that those things which he saith shall come to pass; he shall have whatsoever he saith. Therefore, I say unto you, what things soever ye desire, when ye pray, believe that ye receive them, and ye shall have them." Mark 11:22-24

The Word of God is another tool we have readily accessible, and it is the Word that is dominant and can change circumstances. You have the power to positively impact your life by speaking the Word of God over it. I believe God called His church to be His voice through His Word to the world. Whether single or married, confessing Jesus as the Son of God is key to salvation. There is power in our confession. You can speak life. This means that we can speak His promises about our self and elevate the world around us. We can speak and we can believe what we have spoken. The Word of God transforms our lives. The enemy eagerly and often tries to attack your thoughts when you are alone. I have found that it is quite quarrelsome to combat the devil without knowing the words of victory. Even Jesus, being single, was tempted of the devil, but He responded according to the Word. Receiving the traumatic and life-altering news of my disease positioned me to seek healing from God through His Word which corrects, instructs, empowers, uplifts, heals, and edifies. So, no matter the number of attacks or how Satan tried to manipulate the scriptures, Jesus always combatted the attacks with the all-standing Word of God. Thankfully, I have had the opportunity of meeting singles from different paths of life; some who have little to no relationship with Christ nor any knowledge of Him. I have also met singles who strive to remain fully devoted to Christ and others who have absolutely no direction for their lives – they merely just take it day by day hoping to survive the season. In all fairness, I was just hoping to survive the season. I had no direction. I had no relationship with God. None. So, I understand. There can be tough days and empty nights. Seemingly though, no matter which category you're in, you can declare the promises of God over your life and look with anticipation for the fulfillment of the words you've spoken. When you speak the Word, believe the Word, receive the Word, and you will see the Word come to pass in your life. Get to know Jesus. No matter what you are uncertain about, just ask God; He appreciates your sincere inquiries. As a mother, I enjoy answering questions and addressing concerns my daughter asks. In fact, I will prefer if she asks me rather than anyone else. Why? Because, I want to build that rapport with her, and I want her to be comfortable speaking with me. I want a relationship with my daughter, and more than anyone else, I understand her level of competence. I know what she can handle and when she can handle it. I love her and want more than anything for us to share a special level of trust. God feels this exact same way towards you because He's your Father. Whatever you need or desire, He wants you to ask of Him. It's perfectly okay to be uncertain at times. God knows all things and His answers are true. The word of God reveals the character of God. Utilize this tool to further detect what it is God has called you to do in this season. How can we agree to His covenant without learning His character? He is the same yesterday, today, and forevermore. In the legal field, it's a general practice for a defendant to obtain some background knowledge of the attorney who will be defending them in court.

Preferably, someone facing trial would seek a lawyer who is credible in character. If you're seeking someone to mediate and defend you in your most vulnerable times, you need to know if this person is trustworthy, reliable and good at what they do before you agree to move on. Likewise, it is the Word of God that authenticates the credibility of God.

Date with a purpose. We can at times misconstrue casual dating with compatible dating. We are precious and called of God. Everything we do should be purpose driven and not just casual. We don't do things just to do them, but we do them because there is purpose in it. As seemingly convenient as casual dating is, I must warn you of the consequences. The effects can include but are not limited to, the gray zone leading to an uncertain disposition of either party in the relationship. Uncertainty limits your ability to tell if the relationship is intentional and purpose filled. Casual dating can be harmful and unproductive. Avoid entanglements at all cost, sis. You need to know whether he is a mate sent from the cell of hell. The brother might have horns and a pitchfork. You may need to check on that, sis. If you are still trying to figure out if you wish to marry someday, I recommend you hold off dating until God affirms that you are steady and ready to date. Otherwise, you could potentially cause more harm than good when dating. I have found that even in times of uncertainty, God will bring clarity. I too, at one point in my life, was just existing through uncertain relationships. I've been in relationships where my mate and I were up one day and down the next. It was total chaos. Eventually, I had to come to grip that the only thing holding the relationship together was sex and convenience, so I chose to discontinue because after a while the emotional roller coaster led to an overall unsteady and unreliable relationship. Entanglements are just that – tangled. I've settled for the no title relationships – where you don't feel certain enough to call them yours and put a title on it, but you are too stubborn, timid, and at times even careless to walk away. This is the type of relationship where you just go with the flow and see where it goes - by the way, this is definitely a red flag for a potential bad ending. I've endured difficult strains of relationships, wherein you see the best in someone else and spend the entire relationship hoping they see the best in themselves and eventually begin living up to it, but they resist and refuse. These relationships became too overbearing. I hurt them, and they hurt me. I was tired and got bored fast because they were never quite enough. I still wasn't satisfied after intercourse. After a while, I broke the cycle. I decided to just stop. Stop entertaining brokenness. Stop settling. Stop going with the casual flow. Create my own flow. Go my own way. Try something different. I wanted different. Change sounded good. I wanted something else. I needed something else because, what I'd been doing wasn't working. Through all of these futile associations, I hadn't realized that God was nudging at my heart and calling me. At times, God will allow hell and turmoil to run rampant in our lives, to get us to acquire a taste for His goodness. I didn't want change until I was confronted with adversity and a disease. Adversity can arouse an acquired taste for change. I knew that there had to be a way to win and enjoy my life, but I just needed to know where to start, so I started with my purpose. I believe God allows us to endure hardships to show us how much we need Him. Enduring those painful relationships caused me to discover what genuine love is and the quality it brings to life. It's good to remind ourselves that though we are alone, we are never lonely when we have God. What I want to do is transform your perspective of singleness. Use your God-given tools of singleness to your advantage. I pray that you come to know that you too can experience victory with or without a mate. You were created to elevate. It is possible to be single and win in Christ. It took me years to perceive that in my singleness I can win regardless of facing past losses; I don't have to wait for a mate to start winning. I can elevate without a mate. Winning is God's promise to us. You can begin winning now! You can win while single! There is always a reason for every season we experience, even the season of singleness. The devil constantly aims fiery darts at me in this area of my life. He wants me to believe that being single means that I am in a position of inferiority and that I cannot succeed by myself. He also wants me to believe that because of economic challenges, lack of companionship, absence of intimacy, and peer pressure to dive into marriage, I will never be able to reach my greatest potential alone. This is not the truth. If God is for you, then you are the majority, not the minority because, there is nothing He cannot do. I have been abstinent for nine years and this journey began at age twenty-one. Woo' Lawd! I spent nearly all my twenties without sex. Abstinence was a dramatic change, and during the initial stages, the heart of God tugged at me. Many years I felt as though being single was inferior to marriage and that I had been single because perhaps I was defective. Maybe I was not wife material or didn't have what it took to iron clothes, cook dinner, or do laundry for my husband. Maybe I was just too busy or self-centered, too career-driven, not skinny enough, not this or that – so many insecurities tried to rise and become a voice of reasoning in my mind. Perhaps I just looked unapproachable or wasn't attractive enough. I love wearing weaves, but maybe the good and godly men were more into women with natural hair. My edges were still in tack and on fleek, mostly. What was it? God had to constantly interrupt my thinking with reminders that He created me and, therefore, I am fearfully and wonderfully made. Not only did I have to remind myself that God created me for His glory, but I had to actually believe that I am truly fearfully and wonderfully made; He made me unique and fitting for such a time as this. Knowing this causes everything about me to now make sense. Although my uniqueness may not make sense to everyone, it makes sense to God. And, guess what? Everything about you makes sense to God as well; your facial features, your heart's desire, your fashion sense or lack thereof, your intellectual understanding, your compatibility and competence levels, even the number of hairs on your head play a factor and role in the creative hand of God. We are more than conquerors through Jesus who loves us. Truthfully, I don't have the capability within my own strength to remain single as I am, not by power, neither by might, but only by His Spirit. I pray that every attack of the enemy is cast down and you are encouraged and enlightened on the prevailing power of God. I do not tell my personal experiences to boast, but my aim is to effectively communicate that if you submit to the teaching and leading of the Holy Spirit,

His transforming power will greatly affect and impact your life the same way it is doing mine.

With God in control of your life, even without a mate, you can declare checkmate.

My daughter, Charlie, and I watched the Princess Diaries 2 for the very first time, and in the movie, Anne Hathaway plays the main character, Princess Mia. The audience gets to see the ins and outs of her life; the evolution behind a timid and fearful high school student who survived in the shadows with the intent to live an invisible life of her own. Her father passed away in her adolescent years, so she was raised by a single mother. Then suddenly her grandmother sought to visit her all the way from Genova only to show Mia her true identity and rightful heritage to the throne of Genova. Mia didn't know that she came from a family of such royalty and prestige. And now her moment had come. Her destiny was going to be revealed. She was aligned to be introduced to her purpose. Her entire life was about to change. She was going to be elevated and shifted into greatness. It was time for Mia to be groomed for her position as Princess and future Queen of Genova. After much hesitation, trial and error, eventually, Princess Mia accepts becoming heiress to the throne and is later flown to a new country to learn the reigns. But, to her surprise, she faces hardships and there are enemies that arise to threaten her position as future Queen of Genova. With her grandmother's resilient training, experience, poise and fine grooming, Princess Mia is fully equipped to inherit all that was left to her. There was a scene where the people of Genova sought wisdom from the throne of the Queen along with Princess Mia by her side. They presented the Queen with all kinds of gifts as they came one after the other. When one gentleman approached the Queen, he offered a basket covered with a blanket. Off que, Princess Mia decides to uncover the basket and unexpectedly a live chicken jumps out and began running, flapping, and screeching around the palace. Hastily, the palace staff and Princess Mia chased after the chicken to confine the animal and get this mishap quickly concealed. It was quite a humiliating scene for both the Queen and Princess Mia. The Queen smirks and giggles trying to playoff the humiliation while tugging at Princess Mia. The Queen leans in and whispers to Princess Mia, "A princess never chases a chicken." I laughed at the humiliation and lack of control. Then the Holy Spirit prompted me that we, like Princess Mia, are never to chase a chicken. You see, when we begin to evolve into who God called us to be, we give way for all the right things to enter our lives. We learn to stop chasing things that are temporary and ineffective, and instead seek the Kingdom of God and His righteousness and all other things will be added to us, according to Matthew 6:33. When we chase God, the right things will chase after us. Once God reveals your identity in Him, your priorities will change, what you chase will change, who you chase will change, and what chases you will change. If you want to know the direction you are headed in, pause, look around at what's chasing you and what you are chasing. The bible tells us, that *signs shall follow them that believe; In my name shall they cast out devils; they shall speak with new tongues; they shall take up serpents; and if they drink any deadly thing, it shall not hurt them; they shall lay hands on the sick, and they shall recover* (Mark 16:17-18). Are the miracles of God and His evident power chasing you? How awesome is that! We don't chase nonsense. We are not called to chase chickens! Anything that does not propel, advance, elevate, or encourage our destiny should not be sought and chased. In my past and even today, I still talk myself out of chasing chickens. I no longer chase trends and the crowd. I enjoy having my own thoughts and thinking for myself. I am happy knowing that I don't need to chase drugs, relationships, partying, and validation, because God's best will chase me and eventually catch up to me. I have learned to seek the greatness God has for me and let go of the lesser things this world has to offer. I am learning to let go of anything that subtracts from my God-given destiny. I oppose any self-gain opportunities. Why? Because anything outside of what God has for me will hinder me reaching my destiny. There is nothing more valuable than me living a life that pleases God. I want to be happy. I want peace. I want to prosper. I want to be healthy in spirit, mind, soul, and body. Once God reveals your heritage to His Kingdom, you too may decipher what's chicken and what's destiny. Choose what is compatible and not what's chicken or, in other words, silly. Choose to head in the direction that leads you to your God-given purpose. Choose to elevate. Elevate in thinking. Elevate in seeking. Elevate in securing. Elevate in leading. Elevate in Christ. Let the chicken run! You just do what God has called you to do and serve where He has called you to serve. No more spending matchless time entertaining people, places and things that serve little to no purpose in your life. Forsake the chicken thought process, speech, and way of living that confines you to living a mediocre life, a life dull of challenges, elevation, and growth. A keyway to being single and winning in Christ is to evolve in your way of thinking, speaking, and selecting. Don't entertain nonsense. I once heard that if you entertain a clown, you'll eventually become a part of the circus.

Discipline is a vital weaponry of defense to use while

single. Just a few months ago, I was working out in a small group session at my gym. I'd been out the swing of things for a while and wasn't too familiar with the exercising equipment. Thankfully, my personal trainer was deeply knowledgeable and patient with me in this area. The gym was an environment where criticism of others was frowned on. My class involved a total of maybe four trainees. We rotated the exercising equipment timely and routinely, while our trainer walked by to make sure we were safely using the machines and doing the workouts appropriately. Coincidentally, I had a buddy who I rotated the machine with who compared my performance to hers. She struggled to push through the reps for nearly each exercise. Then, when my turn to use the equipment came, as she watched, she made remarks that I was performing the exercises much better than she had been. I didn't want her to feel lesser. I explained that we were not competing against each other, only ourselves. But I had said something that opened my own eyes, and I said it without really understanding the power in what was said. I'd told the woman, "I don't have strength you think I have, I just have discipline." The only thing that separated my workout efficiency from hers was my discipline, that is all. Then my trainer whispered to me, "discipline is the key to strength". Before undergoing this workout, I never saw discipline as strength. But my trainer was right. In order to attain strength, the fundamental of discipline must be at work. We need discipline. This is why the bible encourages us to fast; not just so we can drop a few pounds for the scale or to feel good about ourselves, but so that we can train ourselves to be more disciplined. Discipline is the core value of strength, and everyone who has achieved greatness has had to start with it.

Because singles don't have a spouse or significant other to catch and comfort them in low times, maintaining a rational and disciplined mind is vital. God urges us to abstain from sex outside of marriage because of the harm it causes, like reduced judgment, potential idolatry, possible depression, and a misrepresentation of intimacy. These effects lack discipline and restrictions. In order to abstain, you must maintain a disciplined and controlled mind. A mind that is disciplined will lead to a life of greatness. God designed humanity to experience a healthy and monogamous relationship through marriage. Making God priority in your life is an important key to unlocking spiritual weaponry of defenses. For God to give you more, He must be able to trust that your priorities are His priorities. I have often seen God grant blessings to people only for them to self-destruct because their priorities were no longer aligned with the proceeding Word of God. They ultimately lacked discipline.

Throughout Scriptures, God enlightens us on the dangers of idolatry which does not always appear in the form of a golden statue or a man-made image; it can also be a person, career, car, finances, etc. Why is such devotion dangerous? Because, making someone or something other than God the head of your life influences your decision-making. We need discipline when it comes to intimacy. Discipline is necessary when developing a healthy relationship with Jesus. Discipline is necessary in order to elevate. Premarital sex has been scientifically proven to weaken our judgment. Scientists have proven there are hormones that cause us to bond with each sexual partner we experience. These hormones are released and can be the reason we remain involved in unhealthy relationships. Premarital sex can lead to disorientated, inappropriate, and irrational judgement. I, myself can attest to the effects of premarital sex. I have experienced the difficulty that comes with continually desiring sexual acts from a partner. At the time, I wasn't aware of the harmfulness of these relationships, because a sexual bond had already been a factor. It's like being drunk to a degree. Oftentimes, drunks aren't fully aware of their impaired behaviors while intoxicated, well, because they're intoxicated. Some scientists compare the hormones released from this bond to the stimuli produced from intense drug consumption. The Bible warns us, *"Be sober-minded; be watchful. Your adversary the devil prowls around like a roaring lion, seeking someone to devour or destroy."* (1 Peter 5:8). The Bible also gives us the key to defeating the devil, by telling us to, *"Resist the devil, firm in your faith, knowing that the same kinds of suffering are being experienced by your brotherhood throughout the world."* (1 Peter 5:9). We have an enemy that is seeking to slaughter whoever he can find not ready and undisciplined, but it is encouraging to know that we have the ammunition needed to remain ready, disciplined, and of good mental judgment to stand strong and fight back. We can be encouraged knowing that with faith we can win in Christ.

How do you abstain after sexual involvement? What do you do when flesh flares arise and where in the world does these sensations come from? If you have sexual fantasies, does this jeopardize your salvation? How can you avoid sexual temptation? What's the point of abstaining? Is abstinence really worth it? How can you deal with ostracization from your partner and friends? All of these are great questions that I am thrilled to answer according to the knowledge, experience, and revelation given to me through the Holy Spirit. Trust me, these questions are common, they are practical, and addressing them together will position us to achieve elevation. So, keep reading and know this is my honest prayer that I believe every single can simply pray - "Lord, if you want godliness and goodness for me, then help me to achieve elevation through you. Help me to win in you. Help me to elevate without a mate. In Jesus name. Amen." If you said that prayer with me, you have just leaped out on faith. You have already begun working the principles to elevation. I'm excited for you and guess what there is more. This is just the beginning. I believe by faith that if you said that honest prayer, meant it, and believe it, that you will begin to see God's greatness collide in your life. Increase has landed and is here to usher you into preeminence. I am overjoyed and can't wait to share what's next.

2. Evolve in Effectiveness

"There is a time for everything, and a season for every activity under the heavens." - (Ecclesiastes 3:1 NIV)

Time Management is what separates stagnation from progress. According to a Forbes article published by Kevin Kruse titled *15 Surprising Things Productive People Do Differently*, Secret #15: Energy is everything. You can't make more minutes in the day, but you can increase your energy which will increase your attention, focus, decision-making, and overall productivity. Highly successful people don't skip meals, sleep or take breaks in the pursuit of more, more, more. Instead, they view food as fuel, sleep as recovery, and pulse and pause with "work sprints." In this chapter, we will learn ways to evolve in how we expend our energy and effort to achieve effectiveness.

When I discovered my pregnancy with my daughter,

Charlie I was incredibly depressed and upset about it. I thought that it would be best to not put a child through the misery of poor parenting, and I didn't know what to do with a baby. I knew that baby would eventually grow to be a kid and from there a teenager then an adult. It was a scary thought, and I didn't feel that I was adequate to be a mother and didn't want to risk ruining the life of an innocent child. I spent my entire pregnancy in my mother's house vomiting and crying and vomiting some more and crying even more. I entertained the thought of an abortion, yes, I did. Charlie barely made it into this world. This low season is what introduced me to a relationship with Jesus. I should have taken the protective measures needed to keep this mishap from happening. But, it happened, and ultimately God saved me through the birth of my daughter. Looking back, she is the best thing that has ever happened to me. All in all, I found out through parenting that the method of well-spent time produces strength. Have you ever felt like you were expending all your efforts only to see no results? It's like running on a hamster wheel. How we choose to manage our low moments and the moments we face when challenges are seemingly unbearable is what separates the tried from the succeeded, and it's what gives you the extra push to jump over the next hurdle.

You are single in Christ for such a time as this. It may help to just take a moment to pause and ask God for clarity as to what He will have you to do in this season of your life. There is a cause to every effect. One of the ways to avoid sexual temptation is to elevate in effectiveness. Want to avoid sex before marriage? Get busy. Like, seriously busy. The good kind of busy. Drink water and mind your business, kinda' busy. To what purpose are you single in Christ? Every season has its purpose. Singleness is a season intended for a divine time. I believe this time set aside can be well spent if managed efficiently. There are many mighty men and women of God in the bible that were greatly used by God while in their season of singleness. Just to name a few, Elijah, Elisha, Anna, Ruth, John the Baptist, Paul, Jeremiah, Samuel, and our Messiah, Jesus

Christ, and the list continues. These highly regarded generals of the faith devoted their singleness to great focus. These patriots committed to their season of singleness with great mental determination to evolve and impact generations. It can be a terrible thing to undervalue and undermine singleness in Christ. Many people think that the season of solitary is confined to waiting on a mate. However, that is an untruthful misrepresentation of our God. Singleness is given according to His purpose and considered a gift from God.

Taking care of yourself and honoring yourself is essential to evolving in effectiveness. What you sow is what you will reap. What you give is what you get. I once read an immensely powerful and thought-provoking statement which simply said, "Stop hating yourself for everything you are not and start loving yourself for everything that you are." God made no mistake when He created you. He strategically designed each person the way He intended them to be for His purpose. I think many times we find ourselves wallowing in low self-esteem when we choose to hate what we have been given to work with. Evolving into who you are while single allows you to grow into wholeness. I personally have had the most eccentric year of learning myself; I mean, I have never felt so liberated. I'm learning that my sacred relationship with God is one of the most precious things in my life and that time is of the essence. How I utilize my time determines how impactful I am to those around me. God called us into a relationship with Him and purpose is something you grow into, not something you wake up to being. It's an everyday work in process, as well as everyday decision making in process. A part of growing into your purpose includes becoming who He has called you to be. Evolve in your identity and who you are to the Kingdom of God. Evolve means to grow gradually and evolving in effectiveness requires your willingness to gradually grow. Be patient with yourself. A part of learning myself, the Vasha God designed me to be, is that I must understand that God knew that growing me into my purpose would be a process. In order to know your purpose, you must know your identity, and by coming to know your identity, God can reveal to you your potential. We must first realize our identity to discover our purpose, and then strive to develop our potential.

I typically celebrate the Christmas holiday with my family. We all eat dinner and bounce concepts, personal theories, and around the world news off each other. We are all outspoken and don't mind addressing some of the controversial topics. All in all, we solve the world's problems while gathered around the dinner table. We typically find ourselves reasoning, laughing, talking politics, religion, and so on. My uncle indulges in the conversation, and, in his attempt to persuade us concerning his theories, almost always leads with his expectation of The New World Order takeover. He goes into a rampage as to how robots will take over the world and humans will mostly be out of jobs. Now, I'm sure you have an uncle or cousin just like this because we all have at least one or two in the family. You may even be that uncle or cousin in your family. I'm not judging. I'm just going to keep right on writing. Then, after my uncle's spill, my brother chimes in to let everyone around the dinner table know that there are monkeys fishing with spears in a jungle somewhere across the world. This, my friends, is a glimpse at my family gatherings, which is never a dull moment. However, through light joking, we touched on the subject of animal adaptation. I, the sane one, posed legitimate feedback about the genetic makeup some animals attain and how at times these animals are capable of adapting to their environment. Now, since neither of us are considered experts concerning animal adaptation, here is an online article by Jessica Hullinger titled "6 Animals That Are Rapidly Evolving" with a subtitle,   "The Shrimp

That Lost Its   Eyes", (https://www.mentalfloss.com/article/64300/6-animals-arerapidly-evolving)

"In the process of evolutionary change, you either use it or you lose it—and this is certainly true for a group of cave dwelling crustaceans. These crabs and shrimp live underground where there is no light, and the sense of sight doesn't do much good. As a result, they've gone blind, relying on smell and touch to navigate the cavernous depths. When researchers compared the brains of these spelunkers to their land-dwelling relatives, they found that not only are these creatures sightless, they're actually losing the parts of their brains associated with vision. Meanwhile, the areas that control touch and smell are getting bigger. 'It's a nice example of life conditions changing the neuroanatomy,' the study's lead author, Dr. Martin Stegner, from the University of Rostock in Germany, told the BBC. It's taken about 200 million years for the brain changes to occur, which may not seem "rapid," but as the Washington Post's Rachel Feltman says, it's 'a relatively short time, in the evolutionary scheme of things.'"

I understand clearly that we are humans and not shrimp, but similar to the adaptation of this special shrimp species, God places us, too, in environments that compel us to adapt. When I found myself spiraling in the darkest moment and time of my life with contemplating an abortion, I had to learn to adapt.

Adapt to motherhood. Adapt to newness. Adapt to the woman God was calling me to be. With this adaptation came the loss of senses. The very thing I relied on to comfort me, left me hanging on a scarlet thread. I forfeited my opinion and my self righteousness in order to adapt. To elevate, I had to be willing to adapt. Our destiny doesn't adapt to us, we are to adapt to our destiny. Often, how we start is not how we are expected to finish. God knows how to best equip you for each season you experience. Although, you may be losing the thing you relied on, you may very well be gaining a new set of senses for your next chapter. Trust Him. Let's discuss three key tools to evolving into being effective while single. I've said before, in order to find our purpose, we must know our identity, then, we must strive to develop our potential.

Knowing Your Identity:

"I long, as does every human being, to be at

home wherever I find myself." – Maya Angelou

You can begin seeking who God has called you to be simply by just being open-minded. Be unbiased and receptive to His will for your life. Life is full of ups and downs, expected turns and unexpected turns. We learn a lot about our capabilities when we are confronted to make cutting edge decisions in our lives. Every multimillion-dollar company eventually comes to grips with making a cutting-edge decision that eventually skyrockets the trajectory of the company. There will be times where your values, beliefs, ethics and morals are tested. It's apart of life.

In 1944, a car manufacturing company was founded.

This company began producing bicycle parts and steel tubing. Eventually, Kia Motors built its first bicycle in 1951. It excelled,

expanded, and began making motor vehicles. Because of leadership forcing a change in policy, the company shut down, however, in 1986 the car company co-partnered with another well-established car company and in less than ten years the company's dealership underwent expansion. In 1997, the motor company went bankrupt because of an economic crisis. They then ventured into many affiliate companies, rejuvenating the growth, and sought to seek exterior designers affiliated with Audi, Volkswagen, and Cadillac. The designers thought to newly design Kia Motor vehicles with a design that signifies the strength and distinctiveness of Kia Motors. Because of the restyling and redesigning of Kia Motor cars, Kia Motors has won the International Car of the Year Award every year as of 2013. This short depiction of Kia Motors shows the cutting-edge decision the company took to elevate above the unexpected turns of life to remodel, redesign, and relaunch regardless of its perpetual past failures.

Some of us can attest to the ups and downs experienced in our personal lives, also. Seeing how the Kia Motors is now one of the most driven cars in the United States of America, despite their early-on plunge and failures, can reassure us that it's not over yet, and we can confidently know that God is remodeling, constantly redesigning, and relaunching us into a better version of ourselves. Realizing who we are helps us to define where we are going. I recently discussed with my younger siblings how important it is to know who you are. My brother and sister, who are both millennials like me, asked a pretty fair question: "How do we come to find our purpose?" Today's society can paint such a diluted picture of overnight success and pretentious lifestyles. I often say that you cannot find who you are by watching someone else. In order to know your destination, you must know your destiny. Destiny is a journey. It's not in comparison to a bag of popcorn that's readily available in three to four minutes. It is soul searching, mind searching, accountability, and transparency. What are your dislikes and likes? What triggers a reaction from you? Your workplace may be filled with amazing people, it may include great benefits, decent pay, and work-life balance, but no matter the accentuations, something will always pull at your heart. This tugging pulls you upward and leads you to believe that there is more. It whispers to you that you were called to live a tranquil life full of abundance and everything outside of the abundant life is pure mediocracy. I have learned great things about myself and where I feel God is calling me while single. I explained to my siblings during our discussion, that God gave us our gifts and talents, and He knows our hearts desires. I am a very talkative person, for the most part, and I enjoy connecting with people. I appreciate diversity and the perspectives of others and would prefer to run my mouth connecting with someone rather than to sit in an accounting cubicle quietly pushing papers. I am not at all saying one is better than the other, but I am saying that we should quickly identify the things we are good at and enjoy doing. Life is too short to spend it doing things you don't want to do. And if that is you, work smart and hard to change that. I know that I am too talkative to fit a role where verbal communication is disorderly or unnecessary. I would drive every one of my accounting colleagues crazy because I am a communicator by nature. I am talkative by nature. It's natural for me to verbalize my day and connect with others. I would certainly say that I am about ninety-four percent extrovert and lean heavily on those surrounding me to extract ideas, opinions, and just great conversation. I may use the other six percent to process my thoughts, but that's all. The reason I'm saying all of this is because, as soon as you are able to identify your interests, you will also be able to identify God's calling on your life. Your calling is like a wrapped gift hidden in your identity. Before we can know where we are going, we must know who God intends us to be when we get there. God created you to be great. Don't feel guilty about that. Personally, I had to sit down and have a pep talk with myself. I straight out had to come to my senses and grasp some kind of concept as to who I am. Who is the me within me? Just like you, I was a spiritual being before I was a physical being. I built up enough guts to have a heart to heart with God to let Him know that whoever He had predestined me to be, I am now ready to become. Your character is the core of your identity. Whatever life-shifting ordeal God has allowed to take place in your life, I pray that you are strong enough, spiritually mature enough, wise enough, compassionate enough, and self- disciplined enough to maintain the shift. God desires to make your character stronger than your circumstance. It's your faith and persevering character that can cause change regardless of your conditions.

Finding Your Purpose:

"There was a very cautious man who never laughed or played. He never risked, he never tried, he never sang or prayed. And when he one day passed away, his insurance was denied, for since he never really lived, they claimed he never really died." - Anonymous (John C. Maxwell)

Purpose identifies as the motivation or the reason something is done, created, or exists. We all know quite a few people who are existing, but not living. I like to compare existing in life to a state of extinction. It's an abnormal state of mind, where we drift through life, hopelessly. I believe a state of extinction is a mentality of defeat. The Holy Spirit unction's us to take a step out of our comfort zone that will positively impact those around us. But, because we are so accustomed to our daily routine, we become comfortable with being full of faith and wallowing in a lack of works to prove that very same faith we are allegedly filled with. If we are not careful, we can easily find ourselves just waiting on Friday to come along, only to see Monday morning again. When purpose pulls at us, our mundane routines cause irritability. After a while, you get irritated with doing the same old thing week by week, month by month. We wake up, get dressed for work, drop the kids off, take the same tedious route to work, stare at the same barking dogs and traffic lights on the way to work. If you have road rage, like my sister, you probably honk and flip off the same cars on the way to work. When we get to work, we park in the same parking spot, grab a cup of coffee, clock-in and wave good morning to the same colleagues we see weekly; we begin working our assigned tasks, take lunch and a few breaks. We then clock out once our shift ends, get back in our cars, take the same boring route from work to pick up the kids, head home, start dinner, perhaps do a few chores and prepare for bed. We may say our prayers (rebuking our bosses for denying our raise or that nosey neighbor down the street) and then off to sleep we go. We get back up by the grace of God and do it all over again. Within a matter of time, we lose our passion and begin silencing the cries of those around us. I believe that God is calling His people to be a voice of reasoning in this day and age. Today, there is a world full of people in despair and desperate to hear from God. The

Bible tells us that we perish because of a lack of knowledge. Becoming fully aware of your God-given purpose is the thing that propels you to break away from the routine and daily cycle of mediocrity. The world is in desperate need of believers who know who they are; they need people who can offer them hope in Jesus Christ. Always remember that people mimic what they see whether we like it or not, so a world filled with people who know their God-given purpose in Christ, will abolish racism, terrorism, hatred, and division. People will see through the life of the believers that God has not left them out, neither has He forgotten them. He loves them and has a purpose for them. God desires that all will be saved and come to the knowledge of the truth. That truth is Jesus Christ.

Develop Your Potential:

"The whole point of being alive is to evolve into the complete person you were intended to be." – Oprah Winfrey

Singleness is more than just waiting on a spouse. Your marital status will not prohibit nor prevent the miracle God will do while you are single. I spent a lot of time on my spiritual journey just waiting for "my husband" to come into "my life" to make "me complete". I ignorantly assumed that I was incomplete without a mate and imagined that, "my husband" would solve all "my problems". He would make sure all "our bills" were paid. This husband of "mine" would just blow "my mind". By this magnificent "husband of mine", all "my wants and needs" would be met. And if anyone would dare to give "me" a hard time "I" would just call "my husband" and he would be such a gentleman to explain that I am "his wife" and he will not tolerate anyone giving "me" any problems. That would be the story of my marriage. A wise person will see that having this "all about-me" mentality will single-handedly destroy a marriage and a good person because of my unrealistic expectations. As self-centered my aspirations were, it's common for singles to over-fabricate the functions of a marriage. I certainly over fabricated it. Marriage is not just about one spouse. It's about two people connecting in unity, together. And, we need to be prepared to walk in that function when the time comes. I knew that I would need to fully develop my own potential before I could properly help a spouse meet theirs. I believe that Eve was created to help meet Adam with his purpose in life, his vision for their family, and his goals as a man of God. Women, are you equipped to be a helpmeet for your spouse? Men, do you have a vision that needs help or is your vision a one-man band?

I idolized this future husband that would save me from

the world. This was so wrong of me, because only Jesus can do that for me, and only Jesus can do that for you. Marrying will not solve all of your problems. A spouse will not quench fires in your life. Another powerful phrase I've heard before which is worthy of repeating is, "Keep your aces in their places." Keep Jesus as the center of everything you strive for and the head of your decision-making. He is the ace in our lives that defeats every card on the table. When you forfeit your ace, you delay your race. This applies to reaching your destination in life. Elevate where you are now, and watch God increase you more and more. In order to advance, you must hold tight to truth and accountability. After Eve ate the forbidden fruit, both she and Adam resulted to the blame game. Adam blamed Eve: the wife God gave him to lead, and Eve blamed the serpent, the devil. Now, notice the devil didn't blame anyone. This lets us know, that the devil is going to be the devil – that is his job and his role. He is unconcerned with who gets the credit or blame, as long as his mission is complete, and the end result is total chaos. Even in today's society, sin blinds us and deceives us into blaming others for our disobedience. You are not single because of the pain caused by rejection, trauma, or a divorce. In order to move forward and access God's promises, we must accept what God has already said about us regarding our potential. The devil will always strive to keep us from realizing our potential.

According to the *Anxiety and Depression Association of America*, anxiety disorders are the most common mental illnesses in the United States with the starting ages of eighteen years and older. Millions of Americans are currently struggling with depression.

I believe the root cause of depression stems from unfound potential leading to purpose. God constantly reminds us that He knew our potential and capabilities before we were formed in our mother's womb (Jeremiah 1:5). He knew everything about us before we did and before our parents knew. Only God is all knowing. It's impossible to seek your identity, purpose, or potential through social media outlets, approval of friends, family, careers, etc... Your potential and purpose can only be revealed by God. Depression and anxiety can become the difference in comparing God's reality for you and the veiled fictional lives portrayed by others surrounding you. Have you ever just found yourself scrolling and scrolling down newsfeeds of social media? Well, I have. And, if I am not careful, I will drift into feeling bad about my life and ponder the question, "Why can't I just be an overnight success too, Lord?" But, the spirit of comparison is not of God and prevents us from developing our own potential. God is full of wisdom and the Bible tells us that we shouldn't compare ourselves by ourselves, because it's not wise to do so (2 Corinthians 10:12). I mean, if we really break it down, it is pretty senseless to compare ourselves according to what we deem as successful. In other words, what I regard as success may not be the same in someone else's eyes. I always say, a good thing at a bad time can lead to a bad thing. A good spouse at a spiritually immature time in my life could lead to a divorce. Millions of dollars without a financial mentor to guide me can lead to a lot of poor fundamental decision-making, if accessed at the wrong time. Trust God's timing. Be patient with the direction of your life and your process. You never want to get to a place where your character cannot sustain you. God doesn't only want to get you to your destination, but He wants you to have what it takes to stay there. It is a gradual process going up, but, a great, powerful building that collapses falls greatly and quickly, and the destruction is seen by many. There is a time and a season for everything and how you choose to expend your time is essential to effectiveness. Proverbs 20:4 says the lazy person does not plant (invest) when the planting season arrives; so that person begs at the next harvest (producing) season and has nothing to reap (awarded). Invest in order to produce. In the first few years of my singleness, I earned my associate degree in Mass Communication, towards Journalism and Broadcasting. Since that time, I've sought ways to utilize my gift and talents in order to effectively impact the world around me. You are talented and the world needs what you have to offer. Those you interact with daily were placed in your life for a reason and a season. Where we choose to sow, plant, and invest determines our harvest and ultimately what we reap. There is so much that can be done and so much left to do. I believe God wants to use you to positively influence your acquaintances, your family, your colleagues, that boss who drives you crazy, that raucous neighbor, and just about everyone within your reach. If you want to receive greatness, you must be willing to invest in it. The sowing and reaping process is all in all, reciprocity. Merriam-Webster clarifies this best by notating that reciprocity is a return in kind or of like value and is considered a mutual exchange.

[Invest in Elevation]

In order to achieve success, we must be intentional, resilient, watchful, didactic, and careful with which how we utilize our time. In the season of singleness, you cannot afford to be lazy. Idleness is what keeps the lazy man from actually putting his dreams in motion. What would stop a person from not planting or investing? I know many lazy people who have great dreams but no action. I know at least two that dream of winning the lottery. They can never seem to put their faith in motion, so instead, they sleep on their bed sheets of idle faith. You already have what you need to take the next step. I have learned in my personal life, that when I take a step forward in faith (not quite knowing what lies ahead), God takes that step with me. The more that I keep stepping forward in faith and striving to remain effective, God sends resources. He sends editors. He sends investors. God will send you that husband or wife, but you must take that first step and it begins with investing. Invest in your future. Invest in your potential. Invest in your purpose. Invest in your talents and your gifts. Every great artist, actor, doctor, athlete, preacher, nurse, firefighter, TV Host, and so on, all achieved greatness by means of investing. You may have a good voice. Join your church's praise team. Sign up for singing lessons. Invest in yourself. I enjoy communicating. I love to just talk and talk and talk and talk. By knowing my keen interest and talent towards communication, I continuously choose to invest in writing, teaching, and radio hosting. We have all heard the saying, "practice makes perfect". Perfect your craft! Perfect what you have in pursuit of purpose. You attract what you are. Farmers acquaint with agricultural associates. Doctors know doctors. It's called the attraction of the acumen. Invest in your appearance. I don't care what's been said or who said it, when you look good you feel good about yourself. This is true. Self-perception and image elevate one's confidence. Exercise and maintaining healthy habits increase confidence. Invest in an exercise regimen. You matter. Christ loves you so much to give up His own life to save yours. Considering the fact, He exchanged His life for ours, we should go ahead and make the life we have worth living. Live, laugh, and love confidently.

Your health is just as important as your talents. If God were to grant you your desired salary, how much of that salary would you need to invest back into your health due to negligence? So, you see, you won't see the results of your harvest in the end, if you neglect your health on your way to getting there. I love chocolate ice cream. If I could eat chocolate ice cream with brownies, hot fudge, whip cream, and a cherry on top every day, I would certainly do so. But, eating chocolate ice cream daily and without precautions, could lead to obesity. Obesity can lead to depression and health risks. How we treat our bodies affects our minds. Studies prove that certain foods you eat affect your brain. We become what we eat. If you eat vibrant and healthy foods, you begin to look vibrant and upbeat. If you select chocolate ice cream and fast foods as your primary source of sustenance, you began feeling down and gloomy.

Many things we enjoy doing can be done in moderation. You may not always feel you have the strength to commit to your local gym or change your eating habits. But if you begin with moderation you can slowly grow the strength to commit to change. The Bible tells us, God's works are wonderful, and we are to know that fully. Ecclesiastes 3:11 declares, "He has made everything beautiful in its time. He has also set eternity in the human heart; yet no one can fathom what God has done from beginning to end." We are the work of His hands. I take pride in my appearance, because, when people see me, I want them to see the daughter of a King. We don't have to wait until we get to heaven to become His peculiar people.

Financially invest in your future. Being single can be somewhat economically challenging for many young adults. Many of us are not as established financially as we would like to be. A two-income household always sounds better than one. Even Ecclesiastes 4:9-12 says, *"Two are better than one, because they have a good return for their labor: If either of them falls down, one can help the other up. But pity anyone who falls and has no one to help them up. Also, if two lie down together, they will keep warm. But how can one keep warm alone? Though one may be overpowered, two can defend themselves."* What can we as singles do to counteract the financial pits we sometimes fall in? A good idea would be to invest and store up. Remember to store away in case a financial emergency arises. It's tough to take losses alone and barely have enough at the end of the week to pay the bills when you are single. Many singles work multiple jobs in order to subsidize additional income. Trouble don't last always. You will reap if you faint not. Your harvest will be plentiful because of your faithfulness and ability to endure tough times without compromising. Continue sowing seeds into that savings account. Be consistent in your investment. Tithe to your church for the upbuilding of God's Kingdom. The Kingdom of heaven is like a good employer's 401k plan; what you sow will be matched if not doubled and returned unto you. God is a great employer. We can learn a lesson from that lazy man in the bible that chose not to sow or invest. We know that when we invest, we can anticipate a richly deserved reward in due time and on time. Keep sowing for your future. *Being rightly positioned financially relieves a lot of tension and helps rid poor decision-making, such as increasingly bad debt.* Be consistent in your financial investments because remember, you are worth it. God did not create us to just pay bills, drink coffee, and die. Our life is worth living. We can experience that wonderful and abundant life Jesus came to give us. All we must do is receive it, invest in it, and reap from it.

Invest in others. Don't be afraid to give back. If you spend this season, sulking over what you may not have you miss the opportunity to be a blessing to someone else. You are perfectly positioned to bless someone's life. Invest in that opportunity. Volunteer for humanitarian opportunities. Sign up to feed the homeless at your local shelter. Tutor students.

According to Proverbs 18:16 and Proverbs 11:25, "A gift opens the way and ushers the giver into the presence of the great", and, "A generous person will prosper; whoever refreshes others will be refreshed." You don't have to be an activist to do something good for other people.

You are a breath of fresh air to someone. Giving doesn't always have to be monetary, but can be transferrable through your time, acts of service, encouraging words, and so forth. It's a great feeling to be a blessing to others. Invest in personal enjoyment. Not only should you save for retirement or emergency funding, but you can also save for that well-needed vacation. Create a bucket list of fun places you'd like to someday visit and begin financially preparing to experience it. A few days spent in Tahiti may provide much-needed relaxation, and you don't have to wait until you are practically engaged to travel. There are a variety of inexpensive getaways that could benefit you. I recently traveled to Sosúa in The Dominican Republic and I had an astounding time. Investing in those brief getaways allows you to refocus, recharge, and rededicate your attention along with your energy. I will admit, you can feel somewhat anxious to travel alone, but, with prayer and faith, you will come to find that there is a world out there beyond your imagination. If you are anxious at the thought of even venturing off alone or even a group of friends, start small. Vacate only a few hours away from home and extend the travel time further the more you accrue travel experience.

Traveling is an option you have to your advantage.

Broaden your horizon. Get up and get out. There's an entire world out there!

I have met many singles who are waiting on a spouse to travel with. I find this an absurd idea and far from what God wants for singles. We shouldn't put our lives on hold and cease exploring the beauty around us until someone arrives in our life. We don't know the plans ahead and whether we will ever get today's opportunities tomorrow. So why not begin living today? Explore today. Master the art of travel today. Expand your global interest beginning today. Sometimes we sit back and wait on a move of God, failing to realize that God is just waiting on you to move. *Cliché, but so true!* Just move. You are single, enjoy it. Singleness can be fun. I'd like to equate singleness to running your own company. You are in charge and are the sole decision- maker. Every encounter, every transaction, all of your goals, your skillsets, gifts, influence, likes and dislikes, what you support and are against, are all a representation of you. You execute decisions and choose who to spend your life with.

Change the world around you, starting with you. Hire good people and let go of the ones that don't mean you any good. It's honestly just that simple!

3. Legally Single, Not Legally Stupid

"May your choices reflect your hopes, not your fears." – Nelson Mandela

I believe who we choose to date will either reflect our faith or our fears. This implies the same finding with whom we decide to marry. You will either marry someone who project your fears or someone who challenges you to become better and accept better. It takes faith to reach for better. I have had my fair share of dating dummies and from time to time, I still do. Actually, to my finding, I was recently blocked by a gentleman a few months ago (Give it a try, they say. It'll be fun, they say). On another note, sometimes dummies come packaged so nicely, but end up jerks. To the majority's credit, I will say that if they think you are really a good woman, at the least they try to be respectful. But, know there is no such thing as a smart dummy. In my experience, dummies will always try to slick talk you into settling for less. They tell you things like, *we have been together so long why mess it all up with marriage?* Or they try to guilt trip you for other things, like keeping up with yourself, being ambitious, etcetera. There are plenty of reasons why it's best to avoid these kinds of guys or gals. But, like the beautiful lesson life gives, it's nearly inevitable to avoid dating dummies. But to this cause, I will say experience is learned. Time eventually weeds out all the bad ones.

I have met many singles who casually date, but don't consider themselves single. I guess, there is a dating checking box on a job application that I've missed. So, to clear the air, unless you are bound by documentation (marriage certificate) according to the law, then my friend you are indeed single. If you aren't married, then you are by law single – fun tip of the day. I met a colleague once, who thought because she had been living together with her boyfriend of ten years that legally, but not quite legally, they are technically married. I wanted to get a blow horn and yell, *"Boo! He's an impostor"*. Why settle for less when you can have the real thing? Does anyone want the real thing anymore? Aren't we tired of the gray area? I was kind of confused and wanted to ask her, how can one be technically married? I thought about losing 20 pounds. So, does that mean, I lost the weight because I thought about it, technically? If you are living together with your man or many men or women, however, you have coordinated your living arrangement, and you are not legally married to that other person with the documentation to prove it, then darling you are in fact legally single. But here is what I want you to know if this is you. Don't fall out of the sky! What does this mean? I'll explain. You could very well be on cloud 9 with your head in the sky and like many false dreams, eventually, cloud 9 wells up and the cloud starts raining. Don't fall out of it. It's easy to forget the important things, your moral values, your sense of direction for the future, and how your mate plays a large role in how you raise your children (should you wish to procreate). At some point or another, you will have to talk to each other about that how cloud 9 will support your future. I have seen singles with boyfriend and girlfriend arrangements end poorly all because the cloud distorted in one season. Just listen to Judge

Judy Sheindlin:

Living Together with

Benefits Chapter 1: Quest to

the Nest

*"Time is an issue, because the sad reality is that women have
a shorter blooming period than men. There are fertility
issues. We look our physical best at a certain age. The Dolly
Parton character in the movie Steel Magnolias noted,
"Honey, time marches on and eventually you realize it's
marchin' across*
*your face", and that's true. When you are a forty-five-year-
old woman who's never been married, the opportunity for
you is different because an age-appropriate guy is thinking,
"Younger is better." It's not pretty, but it's reality. So
women who are looking forward to marriage and kids have
to be*
*careful that they don't get stuck wasting their time living with
a*
*guy who has a different agenda. If you feel a strong enough
commitment that you are willing to live with someone, you
should have reasonable expectation that marriage will
follow, if that's what you want. We all know couples who
are the almost-marrieds. They live together. They share
friends. They*
*go on vacation together. The attend functions together.
They do*
*charity work together. They're together in every way but
being married. I don't know one of those couples where the*

gal doesn't want more than a promise ring. I even know a woman in a longtime living together arrangement who casually refers to her mate as "my husband." She says it's easier, but

nobody's fooled. The men in these relationships are likely to

say, "I love you, honey, but I've been there, done that. We will be together as a couple, but I don't want to marry again." And the women stay, even though it's not what they want. They don't look around for someone else who might be ready to get married. They love their partners and they trust them. They

work at it like a marriage, but it's not a marriage. Meanwhile, the longer they stay, the more their chances of marching to the altar diminish. If the relationship fails, they're out of luck.

Some people can look for a new chicken while they keep the old one in the pot. Most cannot."

I can attest to that firsthand. Have you ever witnessed a couple break up and the guy or gal is in a whole new relationship five minutes after? Yep, I have. It's more common than not where I am from. How did they get in a new relationship by the time my popcorn popped? When did they have time to build a fresh relationship with someone else while with the other person? I think you already know the answer to that. But I'll print it right here. He was getting a new shelter ready while slowly but surely exiting the first one. Men and women like this almost always have a backup plan. Their conniving crooks and manipulators. They manipulate vulnerable people to believing that they are just as invested into the relationship as they are. Suddenly after one fight, he packs the rest of his bags (because she hasn't been realizing that he already had a foot out the door) and moves in with his second chicken. The man already had an exit strategy before the *exit left* sign started hanging. It's disheartening to see this.

Food for thought, statistics say that nearly 85% of the women are right when they think their partner is cheating on them while for men it is around 50% according to divorce statistics (https://www.divorcestatistics.info/latest- infidelity-statistics-of-usa.html). If there are continuous empty promises and two plus two keeps equaling three, you must know something just ain't right. Trust your gut! God gave women intuition for a reason. Sometimes, you will be strung along on the ride until a new ride opens its line. I am by no means telling you to move out or file a lawsuit and wind up circulating through Judge Judy's Court. What I am saying is to think ahead. Think about how your now impacts your future. Because, all in all, you are still legally single. As you age, stability becomes important, safety becomes important, solid support becomes important, and someone who knows exactly what they want from you is important. You are not asking for too much. You are just asking too much of the wrong person. This doesn't mean that you don't deserve better. Marriage is a beautiful thing. Longevity is sought through marriage. Companionship is sought through marriage. I just think that this generation is asking for marriage benefits from temporary arrangements. There is a difference between being someone's long term girlfriend than being someone's wife. Trust me, most men know if you are the woman, they want to marry within the first six months to a year of dating you. It's women, that often asks God to send an Angel out the sky, blowing a trumpet, wearing Chanel, riding a white horse, for us to realize if this is the guy, we want to spend our life with. Women want a sign. We need reassurance and seven confirmations from the Pastor during Sunday's sermon. Let me save you the trouble, investing decades as his girlfriend isn't going to make him value you anymore. Cooking, cleaning, and splitting the bills isn't going to make him a better man.

My sister and I were discussing the direction of her

relationship with her daughter's father. She explained that when she first met him, she knew that he would be the man she wanted to make beautiful almond skin babies with. For some odd reason, my sister told the guy, that she wanted to have his babies. Had I been him, I would have run and ran fast. But surprisingly he stayed. I guess men get the hots for crazies like my sister. Fast forward four and a half years, they were together for five years. The two had a beautiful almond baby, just like my sister wanted. A few years later, the couple wind up splitting. My sister vented to me saying, "I just wanted him to be faithful and I want to be able to trust him." I interrupted her and mentioned, "That's not what you told him when you first met him. You told him that you wanted to have his baby." I then had to let her know, "you can't set husband expectations on a baby father." That's a disaster setup for failure and false expectations. It would be nice if he stepped up. But technically you are legally single and now with a baby. There is no commitment or prenuptial agreement. There is no legal biding certificate outlining his devoted love towards you. She doesn't have a right in my eyes to complain.

She wanted a baby from him, not marriage, not a partnership. She wanted a baby. She got a baby. I told her, "You got from him exactly what you asked for. You got from this man exactly what you settled for." Ladies and gentlemen, we don't always get what we deserve, we get what we settle for. If you settle for mediocre instead of marriage, mediocre is what you get. Marriage holds the other person accountable for their actions in the relationship. Being friends with benefits who procreate does not constitute accountability. If you set clear expectations for greater, elevation becomes seamless.

Common sense can't be purchased. There are social stigma's that come with being legally single. I hear all the time, that singles are not equipped to advise married couples on marriage. I fundamentally disagree and here is why. Let's say that a husband and wife are pastoring a church. They have been married for about thirty years. We'll call them Bob and Martha. Bob and Martha appear to love each other and faithfully serve their community. They compassionately love everyone they meet. The two has counseled other married couples together, held retreats, ministered on what it means to be married and tools they have used to improve their marriage over the course of their years. Ten years later, Bob dies. A year after the death of her husband, a young couple who'd recently gotten married came to Martha who is now single and asked her for counsel on their marriage. Now being a widow, does Martha have the right to counsel the young couple, being a widow, having the Spirit of God, and marriage experience? Some may not know the answer. Some may say, absolutely not, this woman is not married anymore. I say yes, if she is providing counsel according to God's unchanging word. See God's word is never changing. Your marital status will change. Perhaps, your mortgage payment may change. Your slim figure may change. However, God's counsel does not change. If you are not convinced, here is yet another example.

A young man in his late twenties is as happy go lucky as

they come. He always has encouraging words for his colleagues.

His family would consider him, simply put, just a good man. We will call him Darren. Darren is upbeat and strong-willed. He loves God and donates his time at the local food pantry. Darren after work one evening, heads to his car prepared to depart and coincidently sees an old friend from high school. This young woman was isolated and crying in the company's parking lot. She appeared to be somewhat distressed and anxious. Darren stops and asks the woman if she is okay. He also mentions that he recognizes her from high school. The two attended biology class together. The woman confirms to Darren that she remembers him and apologizes for crying publicly. She goes on to say that she would have behaved more discreetly had she known that she wasn't alone in the parking lot. Darren asks the woman if she needs to use his cell to call a family member for help. The woman breaks down crying. She sobs after trying to hold it all together and says, that she is thankful that she ran into him. She was questioning if she should seek help from the authorities. The woman goes on to say, that her husband has physically abused her, and she couldn't handle the abuse anymore, so she ran. Darren then encouraged the woman to seek help from the authorities and expressed that her safety is top priority given her current circumstance. Was Darren out of line to encourage the woman to seek help concerning her safety all because he is single? Common sense would say whether Darren was single or not, right is right and wrong is wrong. Just because, one is legally single doesn't mean they are legally stupid. I'll take single over stupid any day. There are singles that behave stupidly and married couples who too behave stupidly, hence divorce statistics. So, let us look to God for guidance. He will use whoever he chooses to provide counsel. I hear plenty stories of married women encouraging other women in relationships to endure physical abuse and pray that the man comes to his senses. My question is, when will the abuser come to his senses? After the abused is lifeless, huh? I see! Just because these women are married, doesn't make their advice sound.

Dumb is just dumb. The Spirit of God is not dumb. So, I assume (and I'm going out on a limb here because I never assume) that good advice is of God. Good counsel is of God, regardless of the vessel carrying the advice. Singles rendering good marriage counsel if the time calls for it should not be condemned. If that is the case, married couples ought not to provide counsel to singles on how to be successfully single. Correct? Wrong! I have received goodly and godly advice from married folks throughout my single journey. I didn't shun them because they are married. I simply, discerned and accepted the word of truth. I weighed their advice and saw their counsel to be godly and good. I have developed the understanding that diversity in thought should be welcomed. Statistically, diversity in knowledge has proven to advance the progression of an organization/company. This same diversity and inclusion of godly input is what can be used to elevate without a mate. If a married couple were to provide me personally, good advice with biblical principles I would be foolish to not heed it. Woe unto me, as the bible puts it!

For the biblically literate and super saved folks, here is Paul, a single man, who is also a man of God enlightening the Corinth church on the virtues of being married. Paul uses an entire chapter explaining to the married folks how to be successfully married and he goes into how singles ought to be successfully single. If you wish to revisit (1 Corinthians 7:1-40) you may. The Corinth church was wiser than what they get credit for today. Even they knew that good marriage counsel wasn't based on Paul's marital status but his walk with God. I digress! I think I speak for most singles with their head on right and who genuinely want to do right, when I say seeing marriages endure year after year, decade after decade, is encouraging. It gives singles hope that an authentic and loving marriage is possible.

I hope that a day comes where married couples are no longer menaced by the complexities of singles and that although we stand alone, God is with us too. Just as He was with Jesus Christ, who too was single. I pray for a day where married couples come to see that being legally single is a reward from

God as well as marriage. To God, they both have purpose and they both are necessary. Let us seek diversity and inclusion.

Let us all work together to sever this divide. There are two founding sermons to singles. Message one, we are to wait on God (*how long? Wait for who? How to prepare meanwhile? Once we get the mate what happens? This part is mostly left out of the sermon*) and message two, married people don't take advice from singles (as *if singles, are holding poster board signs reading 'come to me all you that are married and burdened, and I will give you rest'. Or that we are wearing t-shirts that read 'take my yoke upon you and learn from me'*). Most singles in their right mind on the right path, aren't procuring in marital affairs. We have our own plights to figure out. Singles aren't seeking to control other people marriages. I have been single approaching nine years and all my nine years of experience with single men and women, the majority are too busy concentrating their efforts on their own lives. As I mentioned most singles want to see marriages succeed. Conceivably, common sense is common sense. It doesn't take a rocket scientist to offer good counsel many times.

Let's just say an old man sees a baby chasing after a ball rolling into oncoming traffic. If the old man yells out *"get back from the road"* to the baby, should the child ignore the man because he is old and hasn't been a baby in decades? How could this old guy remember how fun it is to chase balls and possibly into streets with many cars? Of course, the baby should listen to the old man!

The point is good advice is good advice. God will speak to you through whoever he chooses. It is our responsibility to discern and apply the truth when we hear it. The ability to know good truth and do it is what separates the obedient from the disobedient. Bottom line. When you reach the glorious, heavenly skies and you're standing in front of our Creator, God isn't going to ask you about what you heard. He is going to ask you about what you did. What steps did you apply to your life – your works – what exactly did you do with the information you were given.

I wasn't raised in the church. I was a wild child. I did stupid things and I was a wild child. The beautiful thing about my upbringing and my magnificent transition to becoming a Christian is that I am unbiased when digesting the bible and the truth. I wasn't raised on pass-me-down bible phrases and traditions. Why is this helpful with my walk with Christ? Because everything that I learn is heavily dependent on my relationship with Him and a deep desire for wanting to know the truth for myself. I believe right is right and wrong is wrong no matter who does it. Regardless of the position, skin color, sin, height, it doesn't matter. If it's wrong, it's wrong. If you are advocating untruthfulness, then unapologetically, I shall not standeth with thee! Bye, Felicia! Where does my verdict come from? The word of God. We can't be people who choose sides according to who is standing on either side. Righteousness and justice is unbiased. Making it into heaven isn't like a house party. You don't get to ask the host who is going to be at the party and from there you decide if you wish to attend or not. If you are given the opportunity to go, a wise person will spend the entire day, week, month, or even year preparing for that party. I want to get to heaven regardless of who else is not there. That is my destination and I hope that is yours too. For us to make it there, we need to see good and evil the same way God does. The bible never, ever said that singles are prohibited from providing marriage counsel – secondhand and misconstrued aged fibs has that dialogue circulating. Let us stick with the facts. Let's enlighten others about what the bible says.

I encourage diversity and inclusion. Jesus was single. Paul was single. Elijah and Elisha were single. And all these amazingly profound, generational shifting, life altering singles impacted marriages and furthermore the entire world is a better place because of their devotion to their season of singleness. Being single is not a sin, in fact it is a blessing. This is why Paul urges us to remain single if we can, but if not, we are permitted to marry. By the very fact that he said if you can't hold out anymore, then go ahead and get married, this lets us know that it takes extreme discipline to go up against the grain and remain single – abstain. Many singles (again, with their heads on right and want to do right) truly desire their own husbands and not the husband of another woman, therefore we, date and wait for our own mate. Singles seeking to elevate wait for their own mate.

Paul tells single men and women, that we can be legally single, but we shouldn't be legally stupid – meaning ignorant of God's purpose for our lives. We can go marry just like the married folks around us did. Sure, we can! But many singles who are saved and waiting find it much more rewarding to trust God regardless of the bias segregation we endure from others for simply waiting for what we want and need in a mate. So, knowing, this let us as the body of Christ - all share the same table of inclusion regardless of our marital status. As a single woman, I know it wouldn't be ideal to be in an office with another man (who is not my partner or relative) alone and behind closed doors. I avoid these types of indignant situations. I don't entertain married men. I try not to come off too friendly to a man, when I see a ring on the left finger of his hand. I respect wives. I respect marriages. I even respect unwed couples.

Yes, there are singles who do stupid things like engage in adultery. Likewise, there are married people who too do stupid things, like engage in infidelity and lie about it. The single man cheating with the married woman isn't more to blame than the married woman cheating with the single man. I think we would agree, that they should both be held accountable for their actions. The decision was consensual on both sides. Ultimately, they both portrayed poor judgement.

Once, I was dating a gentleman. We talked over the phone. We texted. All of our communication correspondence was light chatter, nothing too caring or major. We were just getting to know each other on the surface. The guy and I eventually stopped talking within three weeks. The platonic relationship wasn't advancing, so I decided to just end it. The communication ended amicably. About a month after our ending, I received a call from the first lady of my church stating that a young woman called the ministry concerning my allegations of this former relationship. The young woman implied that I was sleeping with her husband. Knowing how platonic my relationship was with this fellow, of course I was shocked and baffled. I thought back and we only went out to dinner once, this guy and me. We hugged (our hug was like a church hug a lean to the side hug - not a full, intimate hug). The guy visited my church once and sat on a separate row behind me. And that was it! I couldn't understand how the young woman got the notion that I was sleeping with her husband. I explained what my relationship with this fellow involved and that it was basic. I offered to meet with the young woman to discuss. Needless to say, the woman never agreed. I sought to find a marriage license relative to this gentleman I'd dated through our local court filing system. I did not find a marriage certificate. The first lady was wise enough to know that the young woman was clearly aloof and misinformed. Legally, I may be single, but I am not legally stupid. I wasn't stupid enough to go tick for tack with the young woman. I carried on. I was able to carry on knowing that this man was not married as she claimed according to insufficient evidence of a public marriage certificate and furthermore, knowing my dealings with him were platonic. We didn't have a profound connection that would cause me to jump into bed with him as she assumed. I had too much to lose. And I wasn't stupid enough to jeopardize it over a twenty-something day courtship. Still to this day, I have not heard from the woman. As far as the guy, he pops up every now and then through social media. But I don't comment or entertain him. It would be stupid to do so.

Being legally single, takes courage. It takes even more courage to deprive yourself of sex and companionship. I think, it's choosing to love yourself enough to settle for better that gets you through. Although, you are legally single, that does not make you legally stupid. When you become clear of what it is you want in life, go after it. What worked for you in your twenties might not be worthwhile in your forties. You don't have to settle for okay when you can have great. If marriage is what you want, don't change that. Love yourself enough to do what is in your best interest and is beneficial to your future.

Equality has always been something that I value. I recently joined a *bridging the gap* panel interview discussing my viewpoint on social equality. I shared some of the ways we can better serve our local communities by first serving our homes. It begins oftentimes before conception or birth of a child. If we want to see wealth in our communities, it first starts within our families. I believe maintaining foundational principles is what helps in achieving elevation. One of the reasons I contemplated an abortion was because I knew that raising a child as a single parent would be challenging economically. Many of the men in the early 1900's (and even earlier), built their homes; they built their families. They did this through marriage unions, investing in their homes financially, and creating generational wealth along with legacies. And those same homes eventually built-up their own local communities. A lot of fragmented communities are crushed because of misplaced structure and foundation.

Choosing to keep Charlie, I knew that I would raise her as a single mother until I met someone, and I was okay with that. I still am. See, Charlie's father and I had the conversation about kids' way before I ended up pregnant. We both agreed early on that we wanted different things. Our values and morals were not the same. We came from very different backgrounds. He and I were nearly opposites in a sense. But this goes to show, two people can agree to the same thing such as no kids, or marriage, and still not take the steps or preparation needed to make it happen. Prepare for what you want – lesson learned. It's not enough to just hope for it and say it. Soon enough, you will need to take the steps to get there. How I ended up? Safe to say, that I've wised up. In the end, I loved myself enough to know that time once wasted doesn't have to be time continually wasted. I knew after keeping Charlie, that if I was going to be a decent mother, that I'd have to get serious about life. Get serious about growing up and adulting. I wanted a good husband with similar parenting values, so that Charlie could see what a loving family felt like. She would be able to see something that my mother desperately tried to show me, with my father. Because, I came to know that, yes, legally I was now single and pregnant, but I made the choice that I didn't have to continue to live legally stupid. I am choosing to wait for a good husband and father for me and Charlie. We have all made some pretty stupid decisions. We don't have to continue in those stupid decisions though. I think it's possible to do stupid things and not be stupid. There are lots of smart people in the world who do stupid. They are not stupid; they just do stupid. There is a difference. I no longer strive to do stupid. I understand if it sounds like a stupid idea, it probably is. It's never too late to say, "hey, I don't want to do stupid today." You may not be able to change your marital status overnight, but you can change your approach by using some good intellect. I don't entertain the stupidity I entertained years ago. Because, I now know, that I am legally single not legally stupid.

[Single and Savvy]

There was a woman by the name of Rahab in the bible who was single, but she was far from stupid. Actually, when she heard through the grape vine that the children of Israel were coming to invade her hometown and wage war, home girl strategized to bounce. She put a plan together to leave expeditiously! She quickly acknowledged her need to negotiate with God's people in order to escape the disaster that was coming to her city. She had enough sense to understand that although she was single, it doesn't pay to be stupid. Rahab was a prostitute. She slept with men for money. She had assets that are inclusive to being born a female and she used those assets to maintain her lifestyle. Do you get what I mean? See, Rahab was quite unique in my eyes. I saw Rahab as a businesswoman behind all of that dirt that covered her up through her chosen profession. She was a woman who knew how to get what she wanted by using what she had. God's people sent their spies into Rahab's city and what Rahab does is phenomenal. She welcomes the spies into her home and hid them when the authorities were looking to arrest the spies. But before letting the spies go, she did what smart singles do. She negotiated and leveraged her way out of catastrophe and social imbalances. Rahab was able to drown out the noise of people that wasn't going to propel her into to her destiny. She ended up negotiating with the enemy of the state – the people of God. She thought it to be wise to get on the good side. She knew that her future was worth living and she wasn't going to sabotage that opportunity because of things she did in her past. Most would say, well she didn't deserve to be saved, she was a prostitute for Christs' sake. Some would say, she was dirty and only used God to get out of trouble.

But my response to that is, wasn't that you too at one point or another. Whether you bartered your body for sex or broke the law in anyway, at some point or another you needed God to get you out of some stinkin' mess. And I'm sure He has. He did it for me. It's easy for us to shame others when our sins are different, but let's be honest, no one is thinking about what they ate yesterday, when they are drowning in an ocean. Genetically, their mind would be on staying alive. It's in these moments we are reminded, that God's mercy is new every morning and of how forgiving God is. Rahab was a step up from a whore. She didn't just sleep with people, just because she needed emotional support. She slept with men and decided to make it a profession – a career. Although it was wrong and damaging, it was legal in her time. Just like today, there are many things that are damaging to our bodies and wrong to do but are legal according to our justice system. For example, idolatry, sex outside of marriage, and the list goes on. What if God chose not to offer redemption to you? Just because it's lawful doesn't make it good for you.

Rahab's ability to switch hats throughout the entire vendetta with the spies is intriguing. Singleness is a constant life of hat switching. Being legally single and having to manage household duties, the bills, the tedious errands, your career, etc. lies solely on you. Personally, as a single who is managing all my bills alone, I quickly learned that I can't afford to be passive. I must be aggressive in situations that call for it. For example, If I am getting the run around or push back from a gentleman about following through with fixing my car, eventually, I am forced to be a little sterner and firmer than in my initial dealings. I must fluidly be willing to switch hats. I have to be as firm as a husband would and as nurturing and compassionate as a wife would all at the same time. I can't afford to be a push over. Why? because, I am juggling too many balls and all of which I am primarily responsible should any drop or should anything fall through the cracks. I choose not to play the *victim*. I take the more *valiant* approach instead. I'm valiant and not a victim. Say that with me, I am valiant and not a victim. If I feel the light bill this month was a bit too high compared to previous months, I question the light bill company. I don't accept the receptionists nonchalant *I don't know why your bill is much higher than in previous times, ma'am*. At that point I am asking for someone who can find out why and by then I'm usually transferred to a supervisor.

God saw Rahab as the strong minded, indispensable woman that she demonstrated. I love God for that. He sees us in ways others can't seem to. Although Rahab negotiated sex for money, she was smart enough to apply that same skill that in the long run ended up saving her life. You are single and have the skill necessary to be successfully single. Sometimes, we are just exerting our efforts in the wrong place. Rahab shifted her focus. At times, that's all we need to do. Shift our focus. Instead of focusing on when God will bless you with a spouse, focus on helping others, pursing your career interest, making the world a better place, advocating missions that hold dear to you. I think when more singles begin shifting their focus and their skills in the right area, redemptive revelation becomes achievable. Light is suddenly seen at the end of the tunnel. Hope is found. Change is evident. Life is fulfilling.

Eventually Rahab the prostitute was redeemed from her poor career profession of prostitution. God changed her tendencies to do things that no longer served her destiny. That damaging career was over for her. And because she was legally single and not legally stupid, God used her to birth the lineage of Jesus. How I see it is, being legally single, God can fix that – He can bless that. But, being legally stupid is difficult to fix. Rahab was a capitalist and she used her cleverness to change her life. She wasn't single and stupid. You can't be both. Rahab knew legally she was single, but she didn't have to be stupid, too. *You can be single and savvy.* Because, this is God's purpose for singles.

4. Single Selected to Serve

For it is not he who commends himself that is approved, but he whom the Lord commends. – 2 Corinthians 10:18

What about ostracization from your partner and friends? Anything worth doing will come with opposition from those on the outside. Be bold. Be courageous. There have been many times when I've questioned my calling as a Woman of God, mainly because I am single. I've often preached and ministered in Sunday services, Bible Studies, and Sunday school and studied repetitively to show myself approved unto God. I delight in sharing the Word of God in any capacity. Many in the 21st century is still unpersuaded that women should preach or teach the gospel. I will say that everyone is entitled to their own opinion. I always take the approach that regardless if anyone else believes that I am called to preach or not, I am to be obedient to what God tells me to do. There is a great social stigma surrounding being a woman called by God, single and selected to serve. I think that God can use single women and married women to share in His Word. If you too are single selected to serve, remain obedient to the calling of God. I had to get to a point of confidence, where drowning out all of the noise became precedence to my walk with God. God knew that I was a woman when he selected me to serve and He knew that I would be single selected to serve. God's provision is granted to enable me to fulfill His plan. So that means that whatever I need or whomever I need in this season, God has already provided. I am still a Woman of God without a spouse. I'm passionate, powerful, chosen, and anointed while single. Your singleness does not make you deprived of protection, peace, or provision. If God never sends me a husband, He is more than enough. I am who I am in God. He anointed me by myself. He appointed me by myself. Being single and called into ministry is service. In order to be successful, you must be selfless, constantly putting others before yourself. It's one thing to be single and another thing to be single selected to serve.

I think that we sometimes struggle with the

misogynistic standards, where single men of God are held to higher esteem than single women of God. Partiality as such as this inspires second-class social stigmas. According to https://www.yourdictionary.com/social-stigma, social stigma is identified as a severe social disapproval with a person on the grounds of a particular characteristic which distinguishes them from others in society. These stigmas can range anywhere from illegitimacy, sexual orientation, gender identity, skin tone, education, nationality, ethnicity, religion, or criminality.

There are several unspoken rules that single women must conquer to be honored, and from my experience, single men are easily discharged from these same social stigmas'. Again, I don't consider myself a feminist. I am keenly aware of glass ceilings women strive to break through, and I think that for single women to be successful they must be more cautious of their choices, conduct, and personal agendas than men.

Understanding how to be successful as a speaker of the gospel, successful entrepreneur, mother, student, etc. is essential. What does it take to be seen not just as a single woman, but a single woman held to high regard? It means setting high standards for yourself, working hard and being unwilling to cut corners or stab someone else in the back to get to the top. Being held to high regards means to be an authentic leader and maintaining a relationship with God. I think being modest in your mannerism and professional in your dealings goes a long way.

"And I intreat thee also, true yokefellow, help those women which labored with me in the gospel, with Clement also, and with other my fellow laborers, whose names are in
the book of life." Philippians 4:3

I want to share an insert from Megyn Kelly's Book, Settle for More:

"Many people choose to work less hard and to prioritize

something else. That's great. My point is simply, if your goal is to rise to the top of your company, and it's not happening, you must look first at your own work ethic and work product before assuming its gender bias....

My general approach when hitting a sexist glass ceiling is to try to crash right through it with stellar work product."

And also, an insert from Born to Preach by Anne Gimenez during her ordination to Bishop as a Single Woman of God and leader:

"At the consecration event, Bishop Courtney McBath of Calvary Revival Church in Northfolk observed: "When they looked for the best man for the job," he said with a smile, "it turned out to be…a woman!"

Whether you are a single woman of God, a single minister of the Gospel, a leader on your job, or in your community, know that only God can reveal your identity, validate, and confirm it. I cannot express enough how important it is to know the God who called you, what He called you to do, and who He called you to be. Without your identity in Christ, it is easy to succumb to labels people choose to tag you with or to be pressured to settle than to serve. I choose to serve rather than settle. What does it mean to be single selected to serve? It means, that you are single, one with God, and that you were selected and chosen to do impactful works in this earth. Also, the reason you were selected is so that you may serve God without interruptions that come with a spouse.

One day I was praying to God for a husband. I felt Charlie could use a great father figure at the time, someone who'd love the both of us genuinely. Within a week's time, I was asked by my Pastors to lead a singles ministry. I was devastated at their request. I prayed again to God, reminding him that I asked for a man not a ministry. I simply said to God, "Starting a singles ministry was not my prayer. I wanted a man not another thing to do." I didn't understand what God needed me to do. I had already been single for six years and felt it was time to move onto the next chapter – marriage or at the least engagement, dating, courting, something involving companionship. I told my Pastors that I would think about the offer and get back to them by end of week. I prayed and prayed for direction. Towards the end of the week, I knew in my heart that accepting leadership of the singles ministry was exactly what God wanted me to do next. That would be my next chapter. I cried and was kind of upset because, it wasn't what I prayed for. Then God spoke to me and told me that I was *single selected to serve.* Needless to say, I started the singles ministry with about three other people from the church. We served in the community, building homes, ministering to rehabilitation homes, nursing homes, schools, young teenage mothers, etc. I ended up leading the Singles Ministry for quite a few years, until writing this book. I was thankful to have accepted the challenge. A challenge was exactly what it was. The ministry challenged me to look at being single through the eyes of God. I noticed what a blessing it was to be single chosen by God to serve Him and others. It was such a great opportunity to cultivate singles from different walks of life, different expectations, different understandings of what it is God really wants them to do. There were three individuals that stuck out to me the most, Lissa, Sam, and Sumintra. I met Lissa and Sumintra at work, and I met Sam in the church. All three were single. When I met Lissa, she was devastated and victimized by life's circumstances. She was battling with singleness because she had been recently divorced for about two years. It was a vast transition. She had a daughter about the same age as Charlie. Going from marriage to divorce, then back to being single has its own challenges. Your entire world is shaken. Lissa would come to me expressing her desire to break free from financial bondage. She was struggling with seeing herself through the eyes of God. Then there was Sam, who hardly spoke unless spoken to. He was quiet and to himself; not considered outspoken or vocal whatsoever. Getting Sam out of the house and around groups of people was tough. Finally, there was Sumintra who battled with depression and anger. Sumintra had lost her mother when she was young and didn't have too many close friends. She was kind but was always willing to give you a piece of her mind. When I met these individuals, I knew instantly that they were special, and God was calling them to elevate in Him. We'd all meet for ice cream and just talk or play games, and I would minister to them what God had given me to share. I strived to encourage and uplift them when their days were rough. We all grew very close and felt confident enough to confide in each other. Within a year's time, I saw God's hand move on all three of these singles. Lissa, is so beautiful and has come into her own woman. She is confident with a strong presence of self-reassurance. She now knows that she is loved, and it shows. Sam is now leading the church's praise and worship team. He has amazing worship that ushers in the Spirit of God. He talks and engages with the audience and has broken out of his shell. And then there is Sumintra who now has a new car and is constantly seeking after God. She also now has the job she prayed for. She strongly looks to God for direction and clarity through her everyday decision making. Sumintra now knows that she would enjoy performing Financial

Investigations for the FBI. I have encouraged Sumintra to walk towards her desires and know that God is with her. It is rewarding to see singles confident in the very fact that they were selected to serve. The very thing God did for them, He can certainly do for you. On the contrary, I have ministered to singles who struggled to attain the concept of what it means to be single selected to serve. God moved differently among the two groups. The singles who slumped and plumped around depressed and victimized saw little to no change in their lives. God would not do a new thing in their lives because they hated being selected to singleness, so they didn't care to serve. Once you commit to changing your perception and once you accept that you were chosen to serve others and not just yourself, you will begin to see God move in your life.

[Voids of Validation]

There was a son and father that would spend every Saturday fishing. The father would allow the son to choose a local fishing pond. One Saturday, the father noticed the son was a little down and didn't talk much, so he asked him what was wrong. The son said a month had flown by and he still hadn't caught any fish like his father. So, the next Saturday, the father chose the pond where the two would fish. When the son threw his fishing line out and pulled it back up, there was still no fish hooked. Time after time of baiting and throwing the line, the son still didn't catch any fish. His father re-baited his own line and threw it, and, within minutes, the father's line began to tug. So, he asked his son to help him in pulling up the line. To both of their surprise, they pulled up the biggest fish they'd caught yet. The son leaped for joy and the father smiled and looked back at him, saying," Son, you rejoice because of the size of the fish we caught, but I rejoice because of the time we spent together before the catch." I think that it is important to learn to enjoy the downtime you have in between the wins. Like the son, we can become heavily focused on the score we didn't get or the bait that didn't reel in any fish. Nonetheless, God is enjoying our constant heartfelt prayers. As a mother, I just enjoy spending time with my daughter Charlie. We can go to the movies, to a gaming arcade, or just an ice cream outing. I enjoy just being with her as much as blessing her with the things she may like.

Voids of validation cause our perspectives to shift to a focus of lack. When we are void of validation, we seek it from our resources, and we seek authentication from people. A void is an empty space that is unoccupied or vacant. When your life is filled with the blessings of God, it is easy to spot the empty spaces. Be assured that we can be open and honest with God about what we feel is missing in our lives; He can heal us from needing validation in those areas. Not only can God heal us, but He can validate who we are in Him, despite the areas that seem to be null and void. I used to be terrible at un-filtering my words about people and towards people; I would say whatever thought came to my mind and would then be completely clueless as to why those same people would be angry with me for saying whatever it was I'd said. I was void of understanding and empathy. It was difficult for anyone to connect with me or me to connect with anyone, because I said whatever I wanted to say to whomever I wanted to say it to. I got to a point in my walk with Jesus Christ where I had to ask for deliverance. I had grown desperate for a change in my relationships and knew that a changed speech and filter of both my mouth and mind would have to take place. These relationships were necessary, close relatives, immediate family members, friends, and coworkers. In the past, I'd attempted to change it myself but failed. However, when I took this void to Jesus, He delivered me over a period of time. Now I strive to look at people through the lenses of Christ and grace. I have learned that we truly can do all things THROUGH Christ, however, we must solely depend on His help to do it.

God doesn't need our help to accomplish anything. Although He wants us to serve Him, He doesn't need us to serve Him! There is a great difference between being needed and being wanted. He knows the plans He has for us and it's His plans that will bring us into full prosperity and success. God tells us to walk in the Spirit, because personal validation is only found in the presence of God by His Spirit.

I struggled so much with feeling the need to be in control, so I rarely delegated tasks, because in my mind, I just knew that no one could do the task like me or better than I could. So, years passed, and I found myself overwhelmed. Now, God will allow us to get deep into certain situations to reveal our imperfections and show us where we can improve. This is what happened to me. I complained to God saying, "Well, why doesn't anyone work as hard as I do?", or, "They can't do this the way I want them to, so I'll just have to do it." Later, God taught me how to relinquish control and allow other people's hands in the pot to keep from burning mine. It's important to understand that other people are just as gifted, if not more gifted, than you. But, that's no reason to be intimidated; just connect your gift to theirs. The book of Ecclesiastes talks about, how two is better than one. Many people who seek validation are just looking to be justified.

Some yearn for a trophy or an award for their

outstanding works performed. I have learned that whatever my assignment is and whatever I am called to do, as long as I am in the will of God, it will happen. I don't need to fight to shine. As long as you are in the Son, Jesus Christ, you must remind yourself that your life is already lit whether outsiders see it or not. There will come a day where every work will be proved by fire whether it is of God or not. Identifying your strengths and weaknesses is a key point in not only growing in Christ, but also growing in the relationships connected to you. For instance, there are certain tasks in life, such as organization or party planning, that I would rather give to another gifted person to work because they are not my strengths. Singles don't need to compete with other singles.

Competition against another person is carnal thinking. Completeness in Christ is matured spiritual thinking. In this season of singleness, encouraging yourself will help a lot. As a matter of fact, I invite you to encourage yourself as often as you can. Another reason why singles fall into feeling void of validation is because they haven't fully matured into the man or woman of God that He has predestined them to be. You must remind yourself that you have a role in the kingdom of God and your calling is validated only in Jesus Christ.

My life was wild. I was careless and just on a downward spiral. I didn't know Jesus or the Word of God. I didn't go to church. My lifestyle opposed the promises of God that I am witnessing today. I am a living testimony of the grace and mercy of God. While my life had been spiraling out of control, God's plan for me was maneuvering it back in control. He has a funny way of ensuring His plans are fulfilled. I believe the access of God's grace is life changing in itself. I recently looked back at old pictures of myself and equated where I am today to where I was headed back then; I realized that God was with me every step of the way. The void I was feeling in my wildlife has been filled with Jesus. I had no clue I would be living for Jesus, and if someone had told me back then where I would be today, I would not have entertained the thought or idea. It's amazing that just a quick glimpse of how God fills our voids over time can shift our perspectives. I cried and cried after I gripped the understanding that Jesus was with me when I lived a wildlife, and today He continues to blow my mind with His wild promises for my life. Total surrender can change anyone's life in a matter of time. God still chose to save and deliver Rahab and her entire household, because she fully surrendered to the plan of God. Both Rahab and I was undeserving of the grace of God, but once we chose to acknowledge our void and admit that we needed supernatural saving, we saw the presence of God manifest.

5. Alive and Thriving

No Drugs, No Sex, No Alcohol, Just Jesus

I haven't passed out yet. I have spent a lot of my single years looking for kings to fill the vacant areas of my life. One of the questions I get asked all the time is how haven't I lost my mind? It's the running joke. I'm not on drugs, I don't drink alcoholic beverages, and I haven't had sex in nearly a decade. And guess what? I am still alive and kickin'. Of course, there were times I thought I would lose my mind; I've even had to do a pulse check! In the career that I've chosen, tough decisions have to be made under a great deal of pressure, and to manage the pressure, some people give into drinking while others quit or find a more manageable level of pressure, and still others turn to drugs. As foreign as it may sound in the 21st century, you can honestly have a pretty good life without dependency on drugs and alcohol and sex.

You may feel like you are missing out on something by going against what's common, but please know that you will be rewarded if you wait on the Lord. This is what I believe! Hard and honest work will pay off. Now, I don't want you to think I arrived at this place of understanding overnight; it took years to learn to trust God. I'm still learning. As I mentioned earlier, having a good thing at the wrong time can be detrimental. You can be alive and thrive without a mate, and you don't have to become a substance abuser. It's not too late to elevate without a mate.

In 1st Samuel chapter 8, the nation of Israel knew that Samuel, God's Prophet, had gotten old and was no longer of much use, so they began to eagerly look for the next replacement. One by one they began using their checklists of credentials and submitting recommendations as to who they thought should be the next king. They wanted to be like the other countries who had kings because they assumed that depending on someone to tell them what to do would make them a more prominent nation. However, they were wrong. The people of Israel were looking to fill a void they believed they had, but what they failed to realize was God was their King. What could possibly have caused the people to dethrone God? Did He not move fast enough in completing their agendas? Did they see or hear that the countries who had kings were doing much better than them? What was it? Why would people then and now become reliant on human hierarchy; on politics? Maybe, (peer pressure.

I briefly remember when Charlie was only a few months old, a few friends and I had a girl's night out. We went to a nightclub and I was offered a drink by a gentleman that I had known for years. Now, normally I wouldn't drink much, but in that moment, I was gulping them down one after the other – I actually lost count of how many drinks I had. Within an hour I was completely wasted. I vaguely remember dancing with another guy that night, and he was a fast dancer, because, no matter which way I turned, he was right there. Days later (after sobering up) I found out that this young man was a twin and not only was I dancing with him, but his identical brother as well. That's why he seemed like such a quick on his feet dancer. I had gotten so drunk that night until I had to be carried out the club by my friends. I was exhaustingly intoxicated; I remember screaming to my friend and asking her not to allow those guys to rape me. There was no one there surrounding me but friends. This shows just how much my judgement was affected. I fell on my face in front of a police officer that night in a gas station parking lot. Thankfully, he didn't arrest me for public intoxication, however, the next morning I woke up with a bad hangover and a headache. To my surprise, my local radio station talked about my public intoxication scene and bizarre events on the morning talk show, but I was too hungover to be embarrassed. In case you're wondering, that was my last drink. Becoming dependent upon substances like this is detrimental to you personally and to those around you. I now know that you can enjoy singleness and you don't need drugs, alcohol, or sex to do it.

To acknowledge God as the head of my life has made all the difference. Proverbs 3:6 says, "In all thy ways acknowledge him, and he shall direct thy paths." As I look back over my life, I realize that God has been there all the time leading, connecting, maneuvering, and positioning me. He has never steered me wrong. I'm human. I make mistakes. When I do trip myself up, I must remember that God knows what's best.

Although God knew that the king the children of Israel had chosen wouldn't have their best interest at heart, God honored their request anyway. The people chose Saul, because he looked like a king, however, they were forewarned that he would constantly take from them. When we seek a king and not The King (God), we set ourselves up to be cheated. The wrong king will only take, kill, and destroy. We know this because, according to John 10:10, the devil only comes to steal, kill, and to destroy. Jesus said that He came so that we might have life and have it more abundantly.

After going from one bad relationship to another, it became pretty easy to know if the person I was with was sent by God or if I had enthroned someone over my heart prematurely. How can we know if we have made a poor choice in selecting a mate? It's because the characteristics of the enemy never change. The devil will always use the other individual to take our peace, steal our joy, and destroy our purpose. If you choose the wrong king to enthrone your heart, you will notice no reciprocity in the relationship. God wants what is best for us, and sometimes He'll give us the thing we so desperately want to show us that we need Him more than anyone or anything else. God is so loving that He will allow you to twiddle and waddle just a little longer in a bad relationship until enough becomes enough to you. It's not because He doesn't love you or He can't deliver you, because He can, but He'll do this so you won't be able to even stomach the thought of returning to a relationship that you know is toxic.

I was raised in a household with both my mother and

father where domestic violence was present. They constantly argued and fought, and over the course of years, the arguing and fighting worsened. I recall one of the last disputes between my parents where my father argued with my mother about a little black book hidden in the top of a linen closet. My siblings and I had just woken up from hearing them argue. We hung around in the living room waiting on the final verdict as to whether my mother would round us up in her car because this had become the typical routine when they fought. We'd leave my father behind and run away to my maternal grandparent's house. But this night was different. I couldn't understand why a little black phone book had been planted in a closet anyways. Who'd put it there and when was it placed there? The next thing I knew, my father pushed a bookshelf on my mother who was in her third trimester of pregnancy with my little sister, Jada. It was devastating for all of us to see this happen. We were kids. We were helpless. It was a dreadful cycle of violence. But, for some reason, my mother could never build enough confidence to let go of the relationship with my father and remove herself and us from the environment. Perhaps she was afraid to take on this world as a single mother with four and a half children at the time.

My mother was a stay at home mom who took care of the house and looked after her family. Where could she go with all her children? All she had known was this toxic relationship with my father, so she continued to endure. I wish she had known that it wasn't too late to elevate without a mate. There are many women who are enduring domestic violence and are afraid to walk away because of the uncertainty of the future. If this is you remember, your safety is top priority. Your happiness is top priority. You are much too valuable to waste years and decades proving your value to someone who, in the end, still won't appreciate it. You can be single and successful. That success may take time, but with God it will happen.

Our lives at times can feel like a chess game and it may seem as though God is delaying the game by choosing our every move, however, He knows how to not only do the miraculous for us but perfect us while He's doing the miraculous in us.

Looking back in hindsight causes me to realize that God has been moving and strategizing my footsteps all along. He has been leading me this entire time, but I didn't always feel it, neither could I see it. Nevertheless, where He has me today is evidence that He is with me. The Bible says that faith is the substance of things hoped for, and the evidence of things not seen. This means that He values our hope, and our hope is what gives us the ability to move ahead even when we don't feel God or see Him moving. Amid hopeless situations, He values our faith. Do you have faith to elevate?

I remember one morning around 3:00 AM, my daughter, Charlie, and I was coming through an intersection. I saw the car on the other side signaling towards my direction, but I proceeded assuming it would yield because lawfully, I had the right to continue. Instead of yielding, the opposing car proceeded to turn and T-boned our car. Our vehicle began to slide and all I could think about was keeping Charlie safe. Instinctively, I turned back to her car seat and grabbed it to keep her from as much injury or collision as possible. When the car stopped, I got out and checked on Charlie and the other driver. Thank God, everyone was fine. I was unconcerned about the condition of the cars but was grateful that all our lives had been spared. In that moment, it hit me that life is worth living and faith is worth having. We don't often consider how, without a moment's notice, life as we've known it can instantly change; a split second can bring about permanent alteration to our lives. These are the moments where seconds seem like minutes and hours seem like years, and these moments test our faith.

I've learned to not place my hope in earthly kings but in Jesus Christ who is the King of kings and Lord of lords. There is no one like Him. He is incomparable to anything we will every experience. The gift of singleness is a blessing. So, we don't have to settle for mediocrity because He is able to bless us with His best. You can be single and winning. You can elevate without a mate.

6. Leaving Leah Lonely

It is easier to give a cup of rice to relieve hunger than to relieve the loneliness and pain of someone unloved. - Mother Teresa

In my adolescent years, I grew up with the wrong imagery of love. My father verbally and physically abused my mother and the domestic violence grew worse as the years progressed. I believe my parents loved each other deeply, however, they had a very lethal relationship. I believe there is a wrong way to love, and I am convinced my parents loved each other the wrong way. God is love, and love is one of the most passionate yet unexplainable emotions we will ever experience. Both love and hate are courses of action. Love is the thing every human looks toward for fulfillment and people tolerate extreme measures just to feel loved. There are times when a woman will tolerate abuse and continuous frustration of broken promises from a man if she thinks he loves her.

It is better to be left lonely, than to live in a constant state of lividness. – Vasha Tolbert

I have had one-sided relationships where I was giving more than what I was getting in return; there was no reciprocation. But, because I thought they loved me, I internalized excuses for them and made up even more reasons to stay. Sometimes, it is much easier to retaliate than to simply sit down like adults and talk about the issues at hand. It was draining and devastating for me to continue in those type relationships; I was unsatisfied, so after having sex, I would go back to being angry and emotionally unstable, not really understanding why. Eventually, I realized that I needed something this person could not give me, and I later found out that what I was missing and what I desired was a relationship with Christ. Jesus loves us too much to leave us lonely. There are millions of married people who are in toxic relationships, and, they are still lonely.

Now the Lord saw that Leah was unloved, and He opened her womb, but Rachel was barren." Genesis 29:31(NASB)

In Genesis 29, the Bible mentions a woman named Leah who wasn't a beauty queen, nor was she savvy; instead, she was unattractive and desperate to be accepted. She wanted to be loved and would do anything to get it. Leah had been single for quite a while. Her father, Laban, had made a deal with Jacob regarding their marriage, but it turned sour. In fact, Jacob really didn't want to marry Leah because he was in love with her sister, Rachel, and wanted her as his bride.

Leah was tricked by her father; she was sold out of convenience. God knew that Leah was dealing with loneliness, but what He did next surprised me. He didn't prevent Leah's marriage to Jacob so that Jacob could be with Rachel. No! God caused Leah to endure being married to someone who didn't love her, and although she was lonely, she remained faithful. God opened her womb and blessed her to be effective and produce children despite her being unloved. Notice how God did not change

Jacob's heart toward Leah. Jacob loved Rachel. But, Leah wanted nothing more than to be loved by her husband, but what God did was alarming. God continued to bless Leah with many sons, eventually leading to one son in particular, Judah, through whom Jesus the Messiah would be born. Leah was important in God's plan to deliver His people, although she couldn't see it at the time. To some she was probably seen as the less important wife, but God had a greater plan.

God is sovereign, so He knows the desires of our hearts. For most of my season of solitary, I asked God for a husband to break what felt like a cycle, yet He didn't. However, he has given me an open and productive womb. An open womb is an opportunity. I have opportunities now that I wouldn't have had if I were married. I believe many singles waste a lot of unnecessary time overlooking their womb of opportunity God. It is God who opens and shuts wombs. He knows and understands your feelings. His Word declares that

He will never leave nor forsake you. Others may overlook your potential, but He never will. Like Leah, we may have experienced loving someone who may not have loved us back. Were they at fault for loving us wrong or not at all? To what extent would it be okay to leave Leah lonely? Before we form a conclusion as to the burdensome romance life of Leah, let's dissect her husband, Jacob, for a moment.

Every so often, I ponder Jacob's background, especially when I'm dating. Dating in America involves a range of challenges because there are a lot of people from different walks of life. There is so much diversity in America. Whenever you meet someone it's essential to take time to understand their intentions, morals, backgrounds, goals, and personal trials. Considering that the men I date may too be running from painful and hurtful situations, discernment is vital. So, I take time to analyze the man and seek God to reveal to me the manner of his heart, habits, and hexes. Dating someone can be compared to a groom unveiling his bride. When the groom lifts the veil, the first thing he sees is her smile. As we continue to date, God will unveil the hearts of men, their habits, and hexes because He is concerned about the matter of the heart.

There was an art gallery where two bidders met once a week to look at paintings from new artists; inside was a showroom with special lighting so the paintings could be richly seen by the guests. The bidders would visit each painting together and make their comments. Staring closely, the first bidder would say condescending words like, "What color did this amateur use on the limbs of this tree? The color named Undecided?" The second bidder would respond by saying, "It's beautiful by design", then he would proceed to make an offer to the gallery for the new artist's piece. Isn't this cute anecdote similar to our redemption? Like the condescending bidder, Satan never has anything positive to say to us or about us. He is constantly at work to fill our minds with doubt and discouragement, causing us to believe that we are unworthy of redemption. But, like the other bidder, Jesus sees us as worthy.

Our lives are like the art piece of an amateur; we make mistakes and our lines are not always perfect, so we need the light of Christ to shine richly on us to keep us in the perfect will of God. You may not feel that a lot of people comprehend your value, but rest assured, God does.

This applies to both intimate relationships and professional partnerships. As I look back over my life, I thank God that all the wrong people didn't see the right in me. God is a protector and, if you'll allow Him, He will reveal to you those who are truly not for you.

The Unveiling of the Heart

*"The Lord saw how great the wickedness of the human race had
become on the earth, and that every inclination of the
thoughts of the human heart
was only evil all the time."* Genesis 6:5

I don't want to just fall in love with an image of a man; I want to fall in love with the heart of a man. I want to be able to trust that his heart is good.

How can the heart of a man be seen? By his continual actions. The heart is a footprint of the spirit. The Bible reveals that Jacob loved Rachel more than he loved Leah and, as a result, the actions of Jacob reflected the love in his heart towards Rachel. Like men today, I believe Jacob made household decisions that fell in the best interest of Rachel who he loved. Rachel held a special place in his heart - he loved her, but as for Leah - he needed her.

Their relationship was convenient. Many years ago, I lived with my daughter's father for convenience. For a short period of time, it worked out. One thing led to another and then it was a mess. Sometimes, when we settle for convenience, we settle for being someone's tradeoff. Leah was never the one Jacob wanted to marry, but because of their culture, the oldest daughter needed to marry before the younger daughter. It was traditional. Leah was a tradeoff to Rachel. How people continually treat you reveals how they really feel about you because their actions will always reveal their heart. Whenever we start dating, our prayer should be "Lord, they may be attractive and charming, but please unveil the heart." Whenever we choose to marry someone, we must remember that we are committing our hearts to that person. In Noah's day, the heart of man was the cause of the annihilation of the human race. God covered the whole earth with a flood because of the evil hearts of mankind. To repeat poor behaviors intentionally conveys a lack of remorse. Am I saying that we are expected to never make mistakes? Absolutely not! But, when we make mistakes, we ought to be remorseful; and try to not do it again.

Leah had her own plans. Her self-willed purpose was to somehow manipulate Jacob into loving her. I find it ironic that Jesus endured similar rejection, outcast, and depravity of companionship just as Leah did, yet, Jesus constantly regurgitated the plan of God to all he encountered. Faith is a language, and I think it can be heard in conversations and in conduct. After a while, Leah came to an understanding, and instead of focusing on loneliness, she refocused on God. Each time she gave birth, she drew nearer to God. Her faith shifted. Through her first son, Leah acknowledged that not only was she hated, but the Lord knew that she was hated. I thought it was odd and unfair to her son to have to be associated with hate all because she felt hated. But Leah, sulking in her loneliness, continued to think that somehow, she could get Jacob to love her (Genesis 29:32).

I think we have all had to pause and ask ourselves what is it that God wants for us that we are not courageous enough to want for ourselves.

Leah remained married to Jacob and gave birth to more children. Can you imagine being married to someone who sees no real value in the purpose you serve?

Could you imagine Leah today just tweeting *just waiting for my husband to love me* or *#Entangled*? Leah eventually had seven children from Jacob, but even though God was completing and perfecting what was lacking in her life, she still felt a sense of loneliness. Loneliness is a root you have to pluck up, so I want to encourage you to focus on the love that surrounds you. Although you may not have love from a spouse, God will surround you with love through other relationships, like a brother, friend, grandmother, etc. Love is like light to a plant. Love flourishes.

I recently had my ten-year high school reunion. Just the thought about going caused me anxiety. I wondered what areas of my life I'd highlight when my peers asked about my progress over the past ten years. One of my high school best friends called to ask if I would be attending the event and I said I hadn't seriously considered it. Later, God encouraged me to attend and reminded me that with or without a spouse, He has started a great work in my life. I attended the reunion with a different perspective because I realized that being lonely is a choice, one that I must neglect. I am loved and not lonely. I am victorious and an heiress to the kingdom of God. I will glory in what is considered my weaknesses and failures, because I believe when I am weak then God is strong and He's strongly working through me as well as you. I showed up to my class reunion delighted and ready to convey the glory of God in my life. I became so excited for my former classmates to see how God had transformed me. I am in Christ and therefore, I am a new creature. I want to encourage you to choose, as I did, to be loved and not lonely. The Lord knows how to deliver the godly out of temptations, according to 2 Peter 2:9. So just know, that whatever your temptations may be (and we all have them), God knows exactly how to deliver you out of them all.

Leah's latter days were better than her former because she began to acknowledge God and her perspective changed.

She refocused on the love of God and not her isolation. I believe that God sometimes uses difficult places and situations to show us our strengths. Elevating without a mate is a conscience effort. It's a decision. It's waking up every day saying *I alone am ready to take on the world and succeed.* I once heard a preacher say that God would enable you to produce in painful places. As God enabled Leah to produce fruit in a painful and lonely place, He will do the same for you. He did it for me. God graced Leah to persevere amid neglect, and while Jacob may have awoken to Rachel every morning with joy, Leah learned to wake up praising God for the life she woke up to.

"Every way of a man is right in his own eyes: but the Lord ponders the hearts." Proverbs: 21 :2

We generally try to live decent lives as humans, but mistakes still happen, because life is full of teachable moments. God considers and weighs the motives of the heart; He investigates our hearts to see why we made the mistakes. A relationship with God is the most important relationship anyone could ever have because we're able to cast any burden or concern of our heart onto Him. Joyce Meyer once said, *"We should cast our concerns, but not our responsibilities"*. I love that statement and totally agree. It seems that nothing really begins to concern us until it is out of our control or completely out of our hands. "You do what you can and God will do what you can't" is a great declaration, but the problem is, we often ask God to do what He has already given us the power and ability to do. In order to grow, there must be accountability for our responsibilities. You must encourage yourself by saying "I am strong enough to accept responsibility and take ownership of my capabilities." I once heard a man of God say, *weigh it out*. This means, count the cost of something before taking it on; consider if you are willing to pay the price before investing your time. The Bible tells us that God will never put more on us than we can bear. When we are overwhelmed by the strain of success or lack thereof, it may become difficult to be effective, however, we have the privilege of pausing, praying, repositioning and reflecting. It is then that we can ask God, "What am I holding on to, or what have I taken on that's causing me to be so overwhelmed? What extra responsibilities have I undertaken that's become unbearable? What tasks and projects have I accepted either out of arrogance, pride, or the need to please people that you didn't give to me?" We know that God does not put more on us than we can bear, but we certainly can. Each of us has a capacity which determines how much of something we can handle. In other words, you may be able to handle something that your friend cannot. I know women who do so much: They're entrepreneurs, sing in the choir, coach cheer leagues, volunteer for the parent partner clubs at their children's schools, they are wives, mothers, and are still faithful and regular attendees of Sunday services and bible study throughout the week. There is a tremendous amount of weight that is laid on their shoulders, and the question is: How do they do it? I believe the key to getting it all done is to give it your all. Make time for the things that you are anointed by God to do. It's unbelievable how many people invest so much of their time into things they are not anointed nor appointed to do. I know without a doubt that I am not a technician. I am very good at single-handedly breaking things; and I mean things that are just impossible to break like a door handle to a refrigerator or a steel pot. I accidentally broke the antenna off the roof of my car a few weeks ago. I can easily break things, but I can't repair a single thing, and because I know what I cannot do, by knowing my limitations, I just hire someone to repair what I've broken. Philippians 4:13 says, "I can do all things through Christ who strengthens me", and I believe it with all my heart, however, I think sometimes the Scripture is taught misleadingly. Although we can do ALL things, we must ask the Lord what things He would have us to do. Because we know that He has a perfect will and plan for our lives, and it's His plan that will lead us into true success and satisfaction. Proverbs 19:21 (AMP) says, "*Many plans are in a man's mind, but it is the Lord's purpose for him that will stand (be carried out).*" God's plan for our lives include others. When we make our own plans, we become the main character, the back-up character, the supporting character, and sometimes the director. Sis, if you are as stubborn as me, you could potentially wind up taking over the entire show. Before coming to Christ, my plans were made with only me in mind.

My ideas catered to Vasha. That's it! But, now that I am

in Christ, I understand how vital it is to adhere to His plans for my life which include the welfare of my daughter, family, church family, friends, and others.

7. The Gift of Solitary

"The whole value of solitude depends upon oneself; it may be a sanctuary or a prison, a haven of repose or a place of punishment, a heaven or a hell, as we ourselves make it."

John Lubbock

I say this as a concession, not as a command. I wish that all of you were as I am.
But each of you has your own gift from God; one has this gift, another has that.
1 Corinthians 7: 6- 7 (NIV)

For a large period of my single years, it was difficult to see my season of solitary (singleness) as a gift and not a curse, but I have learned that it really isn't a curse. Being single doesn't quite mean you are condemned to a maximum-security prison without parole or that you are plagued and unworthy of a loving mate (as some may think). Singleness is a strategic way God separates you in search of a closer relationship with Him, without the distraction of a mate.

Now I know what you are thinking: Vasha, how can being single be a gift from God? How can abstaining from sexual pleasure be a gift to anyone? Is you crazy, Vasha?! Girl, hear me out before you close the book on me, okay? Admittedly, I am still working with God to figure out the answer to the last question, but again before you stop reading let's dissect it together. According to dictionary.com, "a gift is something bestowed or acquired without any particular effort by the recipient or without being earned." The gift of solitary is not something you can earn by works or effort. So, the negative thoughts badgering you with lies that you're too incompetent and inadequate for a spouse are untruthful. The gift of God is given without remorse. Marriage is a gift from God as well as singleness. A marriage is not of any more significance than being single, neither is being single more significant than being married; both are gifts from God. Paul explains to the Corinth church that he wished that all persisted in the gift of singleness, whereas, all would be able to focus solely on serving the Lord with undivided attentions. Now, I pray to the good Lawd himself, that I don't die single. I want companionship, I do. But I want the wait to be worth it. I don't want to get married only to feel like I'm single again. And you shouldn't either, love.

However, Paul continued to say that everyone is distributed their own gift from God, therefore, everyone should appreciate that gift. Life becomes more enjoyable when we determine to fully appreciate the gifts given to us individually. As Bobby McFerrin song says – **don't worry, be happy!** Be happy and sincerely pray for God's best for others even if their gift may vary from yours. Whether married or unmarried, people still need to devote themselves to loving Jesus as best as they know how, with their entire being, and using their gifts for the purpose of God. 1 Corinthians 7 :9, *"But if they cannot contain, let them marry; for it is better to marry than to burn."* I used to read that scripture thinking, "Paul, what are you saying, my brother? I don't want to burn in hell, but I mean it's not like I have a line of solid prospects that I can seriously consider marrying to avoid burning in hell. It sounds like a catch twenty-two here. Help a Sista' out! Seriously!".

Once I dated a very funny and attractive guy who we will call David. (I love a guy with a sense of humor.) Now, I had begun serving in the church and, at the time, I was living with my mother, and was just starting to pull my life back together string by string. Charlie was about two years old. And I really liked David and thought it was a match made in heaven. He made me laugh about everything; he could make a joke from something so minor and I would just crack up with knee jerking, hysterical laughter. Like, I laughed hysterically stupid with him. He was an all-around humorous guy and a great kisser. I enjoyed his company because he made me laugh a lot and was easy on the eyes. But I knew eventually that unless he got serious with Jesus, David and I would have great decision-making conflicts down the line. There was a tug-of-war between my spiritual needs and sexual needs, nonetheless, I did not want to end the relationship. Why? Because, I had already been abstaining for about three years and honestly, I wanted to hurry-up, get married, and have sex. Besides, I hadn't liked anyone that much in a while, so it was very refreshing. I thought if I could just ignore David's deliberate will to not strengthen his personal relationship with God, maybe we would be alright. Regardless of the countless red flags God had been showing me, I chose to ignore them. Again, because, a Sista' wanted to have sex. I confess! Don't judge me! He and I discussed marriage and to be quite honest, the only reason marriage was considered within two to three weeks of dating was because we didn't want to wait forever to have sex. He knew that I'd been abstinent for a few years and he respected my position, but we both wanted intimacy from each other. All in all, I knew that if I had slept with David, I would have fractured my promise to Christ to abstain, so I thought it was best to marry to avoid fornication. Isn't that the thing to do? We were strongly infatuated with each other. In the end, David and I didn't work out; I chose to end the relationship, because I needed someone who was in love with God as much as I was. I liked David enough to let him go. This was upsetting and confusing to him, but deep down inside, I knew this was the better choice. I knew David and I would split one way or the other down the line because spiritually we were greatly incompatible so, to keep us both from experiencing a major heartbreak and disappointment, I ended it early on. I am still thankful to have met him and he has been instrumental in carrying me through one of the toughest times in my life. David used his humor to bring me joy.

Apostle Paul says it best, "if they (singles) cannot hold on, let them marry, for it is better to marry than to burn with such sexual zeal" (Author's version). For many singles this verse poses the question, "How do you avoid marrying into misery when you are experiencing a strong desire for intimacy?" Like me, you may not have a plethora of bachelors to choose from so, what do you do when marrying isn't a current option but the desire for intimacy is present? I used to read that scripture thinking, well Paul, I don't have a buffet of fellows, but I'll tell you what I do have and that is a want to have sex, like now. Like, today! Do you masturbate? What is a girl to do? I don't know about you, but I don't want to marry into misery all because of the inability to suppress my hormones. Just imagine the premarital counseling going something like this: "Well, why do you lovely people want to get married", the counselor would ask. My fiancé and I would stare at each other and look back to the counselor and reply, "Yeah, um, we wanna have sex."

Plant Your Passion

Instead of masturbating expend that energy and passion towards executing goals. Get busy! For it is better to marry than to burn with passion. Passion is what drives us to do what we do with great joy. Passion is identified as an enthusiasm and fascination for a thing. Exactly what does it mean to plant your passion? Planting your passion means to establish it, secure it, and invest it. One of the greatest struggles with singles today, is failure to responsibly plant their passion fully into their purpose.

Passion can be misdirected and poorly stewarded. It is

vital to plant your passion in the right places. Investing your strong desire into the wrong things can be destructive to you and everyone else connected to you. Let's take The Ku Klux Klan as an example. The Ku Klux Klan is passionate about white supremacy. Their passion towards segregation is heavily considered destructive and divisive to the minority race. Unlike the Ku Klux Klan, our passion should be planted in things that cultivate positivity, such as unity, love, peace, and all levels of security regardless of race or ethnicity.

It is important to be planted, rooted and grounded in God in order to fulfill your earthly assignment. He knows what brings you joy and what type of work you would consider enjoyable. It's time to plant your passion in Him and discover ways to elate it. Being aware of your strong sexual desire, as oppose to ignoring it, is useful. Be real with yourself. Sometimes we sense a strong desire for intimacy, but it's not always sexual; oftentimes, it's because God wants to be closer to you.

Personally, I've experienced what I like to call "flesh flares" where something triggers my strong desire and craving for sex. These flares occur periodically and now when I experience them, I understand that the members in my body are at war with my spirit. In Romans 7:23 (NIV) Paul said, "*But I see another law at work in me, waging war against the law of my mind and making me a prisoner of the law of sin at work within me.*" In order to combat masturbation and fornication, I seek God for practical ways to withstand and I take time to evaluate what may have triggered this strong sexual passion. Some would say, just pray. But, sometimes prayer doesn't rid the feeling. So, you must get practical. Could it be lofty conversations with an ex or catching a glimpse of a provocative magazine in the checkout line? There are several ways we can be aroused without even realizing it. To our defense, we are bombarded constantly with the lust of the flesh, the lust of the eyes, and the pride of life. We live in a world where pride, sex, and greed are fortified. These things have become the norm. It's normal to be watching a TV show and within 30 seconds, an advertisement pops up on the screen of a naked man lathering his hair in the shower. Then the TV episode appears again and continues as if the audience hadn't been just bombarded with a sex tease. We could be triggered from a glimpse of a sexual image that occurred a month ago and our flesh will flare up and suddenly begin conjuring up that image. How do we plant our passion when triggered? Pray and embrace grace, knowing that we have a high priest named Jesus who can be touched with the feelings of our infirmities. Jesus perfectly understands how we feel in these weak moments.

Fasting is a resource that can be used to overcome sensual cravings and I highly suggest setting a fast schedule. It can range from any number of hours or days, solely to your discretion. Fasting is good for your body and increases your self-discipline and may benefit you in fighting sensuality.

Finding an accountability partner with whom you can discuss these weaknesses may be helpful as well. Consulting with a trusted friend or peer is a resourceful way to appropriately plant your passion. James 5:16 says, "*Therefore confess your sins to each other and pray for each other so that you may be healed. The prayer of a righteous person is powerful and effective.*" As Whodini says in the song titled Friends, "*Friends, how many of us have them. Friends, ones we can depend on?*" Count on your friends. That's what they are there for. Use them! Rely on the counsel God has placed in your life through your friends. It's okay to ask for help, advice, or guidance.

Protect Your Passion

Every person, whether single or married, should have something that they are passionate about. Protecting your passion is critical because we have an adversary, the devil, who wants to pervert our passion. His desire is to take what God meant to cultivate goodness and turn that potential into something damaging. For example, a person may be a visionary who is creative and can create something out of nothing but an imagination, but the devil can plant a seed of pornography in his/her heart and that person's passion is misplaced. Early in my season of singleness, I was passionate about a lot of things like fashion, music, advocating, sewing, and I am still passionate about quite a few things.

What helped me protect my passions was to take inventory of all the things I could do and make a list prioritizing them from the things I liked best to the things I liked least. Why is it important to know the difference? Because, if we're not careful, we will spend a lot of time passionate about things that aren't producing results. If you aren't sure of which things you do well, find a friend or relative to ask, but be sure you ask someone who, without a doubt, will be truthful, not sparing your feelings. There are many people who enjoy singing but are terrible singers. They make an entire audience shrink in awkwardness and their performance is painful. There are people who aren't great managers and it shows through high turn-over rates. These two scenarios are situations for disasters. People sometimes spend years doing things they like but really aren't good at, and because they don't have the guts to own up to the fact that they're not good at it, they end up not helping themselves or anyone else. So, what happens? The people listening to the awful singer don't enjoy it and the manager is forcing his subordinates to either leave or remain stagnant because there are limited to no growth opportunities.

By listing my passions according to priority, I was able to focus and protect them. You cannot protect what you don't prioritize. Not only does this list help prioritize my life, but it also helps to protect and prioritize my family. My gift to teach and share the word of God is at the top of my list, therefore, I will invest in it with or without a paycheck. Accountability starts with understanding that we make time for the things we want. In order to live a passionate life, we must prioritize and protect our God-given passions.

Prove Your Passion

If you have ever been to Sunday school, I'm sure you have read or heard the story of David and Goliath the giant. Then you know, that David killed Goliath in the valley while the rest of David's companion soldiers camped on the side of the mountain. David proved his passion in slaying this giant. When our passion is properly managed, it will prove our hard work, and the late nights spent practicing for perfection.

My father is glorified and honored by this, when you bear much fruit, and prove yourselves to be My true disciples. (John 15:8)

Everything we do, and our beliefs and values will be proven. Fuel your purpose with your passion for things that will bring God glory. In your season of singleness, I encourage you to commit to your purpose. Proving your passion is when you can go through trials, turbulence, and times of testing yet you remain faithful to your purpose.

I am a working mother so finding time to operate and excel in my passion was challenging. When God gave me the vision of becoming an author and sharing my story with the world, there were so many excuses I could have made for not starting, like not being ready or not having enough time, or, that

I am a single mother and I don't have the resources necessary. But instead, I began to prove my passion to God because I wanted others to experience the abundant life, He promised to them. I sought to prove that I do believe that all things work together for my good even when I don't feel like anything I try to do is working. I made up my mind to step out on faith and make time for the things God has called me to do. I started prioritizing, utilizing my lunch breaks to write in a conference room that I booked at work to give me uninterrupted time and space. After work, I exercised, and once a week I attended Bible study and choir rehearsal; I spent time with Charlie, and before bedtime, I enforced marketing tools and activities for our singles monthly meeting. I was no longer as drained, and I began to make more and more mild accomplishments. Sometimes, all we need to do is reschedule our daily routine. Suddenly, I had the time, resources, and the opportunity, once I started shifting my schedule. I became more intentional about the usage of my time. What are some ways you can properly utilize the gift of solitary?

I believe that when we see the gift of solitary as a gift and not grief, we will then maximize our capabilities. Resources will become available. Opportunities will begin lining up.

I also believe that God allows us to experience a season of solitary so we may grow to fully understand the depth of Christ's love toward us. Remember, we love God, because He first loved us, not the other way around. God chose to prove His love toward us through the death and resurrection of Jesus Christ. He casted His pure love on us through His grace. God loves us for who we are, where we are, and why we are; He even knows why we are the way we are. Others may misunderstand, but Jesus knows and definitely understands. It warms my heart to know that He loves me without explanation, and He chooses to love me despite my faults. Sis, you can experience this same type of love. All you must do is believe in Him and accept the fact that He already loves you. You don't have to apply MAC to be loved by Him. You don't have to brush your hair perfectly to be valued. You don't have to slip on your red bottoms to elevate without a mate. Believing earnestly, that He loves you is the building foundation to healing every facet of your life. Did you know that God even cares about every one of your relationships because He wants the best life for you?

But if you harbor bitter envy and selfish ambition in your hearts, do not boast about it or deny the truth. Such "wisdom" does not come down from heaven but is earthly, unspiritual, demonic. James 3:14-15

I am frequently asked questions like, "What do you do when your cravings or passions are turned from godly things to ungodly fulfilment?" Or, "Is it possible to be a Christian and have sensual longings?" My answer is, "Absolutely, yes!" How would I know? Because I have been there. When I find myself wanting things that are harmful to me, I pray and assess my walk with Christ. Doing this will help avoid engaging in wrongful acts or falling into temptation. It keeps me from randomly sleeping with Joe Smoe from around the corner. When we hear the term "falling into temptation" we may visualize someone falling 1200 feet off a cliff into a vast black sea at midnight, yelling "Help, I'm falling!" or we may think of the television commercial where the elderly woman falls in her home and screams, " Help, I have fallen and I can't get up." Just like the elderly woman, Jesus is one alert button press away. He will help you up in your time of need whether your fall is 200 feet or 1200 feet. It doesn't take a lot to fall into temptation because the devil is subtle and so are his schemes and devices, but the love of God can reach you no matter the depth of your fall. All you need to do is cry out, "HELP!"

This is the reason why it's best to immediately confront your hidden battles. Periodically, I check my daily prayer life routine: Am I talking to God as often as I should? Are new relationships influencing me in ungodly ways? Have I slacked in attendance with my local church? Am I distracted by bills, relational issues, my career, and other things of this world? I do a thorough routine check, and anything contrary is confronted, challenged and corrected. Sometimes we are our biggest critics, and although this may be dreadful it can serve a great purpose. When we choose to strongly critique and challenge ourselves to stay in alignment with God's will and His Word, we can prevent hindrances. Let's be honest, we know when we are messing up long before others see it and by the time there is intervention or an AA meeting established to help get our lives back on track, the situation is more difficult. Sin is like an oil-stain on fabric; over time it becomes more evident to the eye and at times permanent. Choose to become intolerable of dead pits because, we were made to walk over them and not waddle in them.

"Anna was a prophetess who'd lived with her husband for seven years of her life. Her husband died. She remained widowed for eighty years." Luke 2:36-39

Luke chapter 2 introduces us to a phenomenal woman by the name of Anna who was effective in her season of singleness and utilized her gift of solitary to her advantage. Whatever the key was to remaining single and abstinent, Anna used it. She remained in the presence of the Lord worshipping, fasting, and praying day and night. Now, I am certainly not advising that you quit your job, abandon your family, and go on a heaven climbing hiatus, wearing sheep skin, because God doesn't require that in most cases. But what this scenario implies is that longing for the presence of God can be a gateway to minimizing temptation.

I have ministered to several singles who truly in their hearts desire to remain abstinent and avoid sex outside of marriage, but it's difficult for them, and, of course, I understood. And I have learned that marriage requires work, and it is better to wait long than to marry wrong. Spiritual rituals are helpful as well because they allow for a more disciplined and routine prayer life, fasting agenda, and worship. Although spiritual rituals are beneficial, they are not required for salvation. Accepting Jesus Christ as your Lord and personal Savior opens the door to salvation, whereas spiritual rituals aid in developing your relationship with Him and allows for routine meditation and devotion toward God. Knowing that there are substantial trials and adversities that we must face in this season of singleness, I have learned to set my affection on the eternal lasting things and not temporary things this world has to offer. I now understand that God is the source of every supply and solution to every demand we face.

The seasons of our lives will change, and Anna had experienced such change, going from marriage to celibacy after becoming a widow. We must position ourselves to embrace change because nothing stays the same. You can be as poor as dirt one year and listed in Forbes Magazine as the wealthiest person on earth the following year. There are countless testimonies of couples trying hard to have children but are infertile. Then, before you know it, they are sending invites to Little James Jr.'s first birthday party. What I am saying is that situations are subject to change, but our source should remain the same. Considering the many years Anna was actively engaged in solitary, I now understand how important perspective is to everything that takes place in our lives. Our perspective evolves from our way of thinking, the way we treat people, our work ethics, our social endeavors, and so on and so forth. I recall having the wrong perspective; how I perceived myself and chose to handle people and circumstances derived from my own outlook. I had a putrid insight and could argue down a lawyer if I believed my way was the right way. People eventually stopped caring to be around me because my perception of things and people drove everyone that cared for me away. It wasn't until I became filled with the Holy Spirit, that God started showing me how jacked up my outlook on a lot of things was, so I began to intentionally pursue good thinking – letting go of empty thoughts that had held me captive for so long; they were now being removed from my knowledge base.

The Word of God encourages us to think on good things and to set our affection on things above - eternal things - and not things below or here on earth. If we decide to set our unravelling affection on the things and ways of this world, it will ultimately drive us anxious and just plain crazy.

I have crossed paths with singles who long to control every aspect of their walk with God and compromise their purity for counterfeit relationships without first learning how to coordinate their affection fittingly. Love works when we align our affection upwardly and not solely outwardly. A moment of celebration and jubilee happens when we have both the vertical and horizontal love of the Father; this is the love Christ exemplified on the cross. Heavenly affection divinely connects us to the assignment of heaven and teaches us how to experience the kingdom of God here on earth. *"As a man thinks in his heart so is he."* One exercise that propelled my faith in God and my faith in this gift of solitary was to allow God to reconstruct how I thought about myself. It is important to run towards becoming the man or woman God has called you to be rather than cowering from it. I reached a pinnacle where I needed a new image of myself. I needed to know the new, soft heart God had given me, no longer the heart of stone. I needed to rekindle a fire and love for myself. I found out that in order to press forward into a new destiny, I had to be restored, rebuilt, and renewed. It wasn't going to work unless I sought God and came into agreement with the calling He'd placed on my life before He formed me in the womb of my mother. Who is this Woman of God, Vasha

Tolbert? What does she look like? What are her values? What manner of people respect her and why? What is her purpose? What are some admirable traits about her characteristics? Is her speech flamboyant and seasoned with grace? Who is she?

Now the question is, who are you? If, you have a moment, go ahead and answer those same questions about you, the new you in God and all that you are becoming. You reach a pivotal point in your faith where in order to cross over into your promised land, you must learn to see the provision in the rock before striking it. When Moses was instructed by God to strike the rock, God was teaching him how to access the promise land through a new mindset - a new perspective. God had the infallible power to make a river flow from anything in the wilderness, but He chose to perform a miracle through a dry rock. This proves He can use something as ordinary and common as a rock to quench the thirst of an entire nation. A rock and water are opposite elements; water flows while a rock is a solid, dry substance. Water can be used to cleanse and purify whereas a rock is so dry, that it can ignite a fire. I love how God can take two different things with little to no commonalities and prove His almighty power.

In the beginning stages of solitary or singleness we may see ourselves as common and ordinary as a rock, but when you begin to elevate in singleness, God will use your rock to spring forth water and flourish the lives of many. We are rivers of living water that God wants to use in dry places, bringing restoration to the lives of people all around us. Elevation is personal development; it's continuous unveiling of yourself. It's imperative that we don't take singleness for granted and that we understand the importance of not being influenced by relatives or peers to do things we weren't created to do. Yes, the Word of God says we can do all things through Christ who strengthens us, but wisdom teaches us that just because you CAN doesn't mean you were CALLED to do it.

I am complete in Christ, and though I am alone, I am not lonely because God promised He'd never leave nor forsake me. In those times when you feel lonely, encourage yourself knowing that Christ is with you, developing and shaping you into a better version of yourself. Elevation is seeing the hand of God operate in your life in remarkable and even extraordinary ways. So, I challenge you to enjoy the gift of solitary and make the most of it; use this personal time to flourish.

This brings me to my next point. A few days ago, I went to exercise with my mom and sisters, and as we were walking in the middle of the road, I noticed grass growing amid concrete asphalt. I did what every other millennial would do – I stopped and took a picture of the grass that had grown in the middle of a concrete road. In that moment, the Holy Spirit revealed to me that no matter what season we find ourselves in, Christ can allow us to produce. If we are a seed planted in a garden, we are to produce. If he chooses to plant us amongst a riverbed, we are to produce. When we are planted in a workplace that lacks integrity and the pay is unfavorable, we are to produce. In the midst of a divorce, we can produce. When rejection is delivered in the mail, we can produce. If the test results are unpleasant, produce. Regardless to the situation, rise above it. It amazed me that grass would grow in a hard place, but it did. That's the same expression that light gives in a dark world. When others see that life has planted us in trivial places, yet we continue to produce and elevate, they are drawn to our redeemer, Jesus Christ. The choice is yours. I made my decision to elevate years ago. Will you produce or live a life barren? Jesus showed us this example using a fig tree. He was returning from a journey and was hungry, so he fixed His expectation on a fig tree. When He approached it, there was no fruit to eat. His disappointment caused Him to curse the tree which shortly thereafter withered and died. The Bible didn't specify exactly why the tree was barren, but just that it was unfruitful. Regardless to how long we are single, we are to continue to bear fruit and elevate. We all have been like this fig tree at one point or another – barren and unproductive. Although the fig tree grew in stature, it didn't produce fruit, so it was not fulfilling its purpose because it was designed to feed others. God desires that we prosper and be in good health even as our soul prospers, and there is no limit as to how you can grow in God. In the world what appears to be fruit may oftentimes be fraudulent and not lasting fruit. It is the will of God that you continue to bear fruit and prosper in every aspect of your life. Anna unlocked the key to a truly content and fulfilling life, and it was through her contentment and faithfulness that she witnessed the promised Son of God – Jesus, who takes away the sins of the world. How do you bear fruit in solitary? Trust the process. Trust the procedure. Trust the production. Trust God. Work while you wait.

The Lord said, "It is not good for the man to be alone. I will make a helper suitable for him." Genesis 2:18 (NIV)

"Well, God, if it is not good that I am single, then why haven't I met a suitable mate? Why are there still singles in Christ?" God first created Adam and then Eve who would suffice Adam's lack of human companionship. The question as to why God decided to create us with a deficit in companionship has always been a running inquiry in my mind. After all, Adam was made in the image and likeness of God, Jesus, and the Holy Spirit, and even though he was like God, he was still human, personifying both humanity and divinity according to God's purpose. We were made in the image of God, which makes us like Him, but we are not God because of the very essence of our human nature. Yet, God has made everything beautiful in its time, according to Ecclesiastes 3:11. Notwithstanding, Adam's deficit derived from being alone and lacking a comparable companion. The time he spent single, unaccompanied, and isolated was beautiful in its own time. Singleness is a beautiful thing in its own time. There is a time to refrain from embracing, companionship, and basking in the exhilaration of a loved one, and although troubles are experienced through isolation, negligence of intimacy, or affection, these experiences can produce in you fruit that you will need for an upcoming season.

No, it's not good to be alone, but your time is coming,

and the same fruit God produced in Adam through singleness of thought, body, spirit, heart, soul, and mind is what He is currently producing in you. Will your tree be full of good fruit when your season of singleness is concluding? Or will you be barren because you were too impatient to wait and grow? The pains of lonely nights and the absence of *good morning calls* and *heart eye emoji texts* is all working for your good. Why?

Because, God has made everything beautiful for its own time. Knowing this you can now enjoy the moment of each day, understanding that each moment manifests progress. Once again, trust the process. Trust the procedure. Trust the production. Trust God. Work while you wait.

In order to become a better version of yourself, you must trust the procedure, gain insight from it and, trust that God is producing a far more greater thing in you. Adam was deficit of companionship and a helpmeet, however, he was winning while single; he mastered singleness without a mate. His singleness allowed him time to be groomed into a leader. Although he was isolated, he experienced an up-close and personal relationship with God who was teaching him how to be a blessing and not a curse to his future wife, Eve. God talked with Adam, giving him divine instructions for his life. He delegated authority to Adam and taught him how to manage what was given to him. Adam was at liberty to explore the lofty terrain of the land; he was single and allowed to create, steward, and construct. God created the trees in the earth at seed form and instructed them to begin the reproduction process. The seed would eventually grow into trees and create a cycle of reproducing trees. Nevertheless, when God formed Adam, he formed a man not a child, and although he was very much an adult, he still required grooming and growth. This teaches singles to remain coachable in this season.

It comforts me to know that God does not heavily focus on the outer appearance of man, but He really examines the heart. Sometimes we can see the exterior of others and think that they have mastered a certain level of maturity in their life, but God, who looks intently and with compassion at our hearts understands that we still require grooming and growth. If he sends your spouse while your heart has not quite healed to receive or give love, you will sabotage it. Remember, beloved, a good thing given at the wrong time can still be a bad thing. I challenge you to search your heart and ask yourself these questions, "Have I mastered the art of singleness? Am I discontented and impatient? Am I ready to give and receive love? How can I become a better version of myself, in order to be a better spouse to someone else? What are my priorities right now? How am I leading in this season? How effective am I in my community at this time? Who have I helped?"

In the book of Genesis, the land produced vegetation: plants bearing seed according to their kind and trees bearing fruit with seed according to its kind. And God saw that it was good. Are you operating from a barren and empty place? Do you exemplify all the qualities you are expecting from your future spouse? How much of this season have you spent dating yourself? Is self-love visible in your life? How are you treating others? Make sure you are producing good fruit; that you are elevating and not relegating. How would you know for certain?

Because, fruit is attractive. It's radiant. It's an upward slope of optimism. If your tree is unproductive, get to the root of the problem and don't be afraid to pluck it up!

Photosynthetic proves that seeds endure a process, they encounter trials according to a reproductive procedure, and ultimately grows into a far greater thing. Hang in there; God's got you! Will you trust Him? Don't shut love out. Give the devil no foothold to keep you from enjoying agape love and interaction.

I believe healthy relationships are essential to elevating, so go-ahead girl, plan a movie night with a friend or setup a brunch with a co-worker. The Word of God tells us that the wealth of the wicked is laid up for the righteous. My interpretation of this is that there is a surplus of wealth that comes through relationships. Having good people in your life, is amazing. So cultivate those friendships and maintain thriving relationships.

I believe when God promises to bless you with wealth, it not only refers to monetary increase, but a surplus wealth of like- minded relationships, a wealth of knowledge, a wealth of intellect, a wealth of insight, and the list continues. This is the abundant life Jesus came to give. Start enjoying it. Moreover, this wealth, is laid up for you! Trust me, I completely understand the frightening feeling of opening yourself up to others. The troublesome thought of sharing your space, goals, ideas, and trials with another individual can make anyone anxious, especially if you are unaware of their true motives and intents. It can be bothersome trying to decipher if their acts of kindness and level of commitment to your friendship is from a goodhearted place. At one point in time, I shut out nearly everyone when distress knocked at my door. I didn't want to give anyone access to my vulnerability, so, I had no interest in connecting with social groups. I left church services immediately upon dismissal, simply because I rejected fellowship. I refused the small church chat after service about how good the pastor preached and the amazing praise and worship, and how the Spirit of God moved in *Sister White Socks*. I didn't care to extend a third hug to *Deacon*

Peppermint. I completely had no interest in fostering a thriving relationship with anyone around me. I would immediately leave service and literally be out of the parking lot within sixty seconds, leaving tire marks smeared on the concrete. To my defense, I was broken at that time. I had faced an incurable disease that I didn't feel comfortable disclosing to church folk or anyone else for that matter. Because my life was shattered like a mirror, I no longer saw my reflection. It's difficult to perceive your identity in a shattered mirror because your reflection is distorted. Since I had become greatly discouraged because of the disease, I no longer had the capacity necessary to foster friendships, and because I no longer saw myself or knew my purpose, it became problematic to understand the good in inviting someone else into my life. I used that time alone to talk with God. It became essential to learn myself and learn the character and true nature of God. Eventually, I was able to step out of my shell and interact with others. I am now at a point where I make it a priority to connect and build relationships.

As singles, we can subject ourselves to isolation so easily, but I have learned that we must make a conscious effort towards self-love and improvement. We must also make conscious efforts to take care of our bodies through exercising and eating healthy, connect and grow godly and good relationships, and seize moments of opportunity. Had I not consciously tried to grow and nourish godly and meaningful relationships in my life, I wouldn't have positioned myself to see the hand of God move through people on my behalf. God wants to bless you through others, however, it's difficult to see this when you are closed off from the world. It's fine to be single in the gift of solitary, but, God did not call His people to isolation for long periods of time. Even Elijah and Elisha who were single prophets conversed with people ranging from widows to kings. These prophets of God experienced the gift of solitary and edified others in their singleness. I challenge you to positively impact lives in your season of solitary. For those desiring to be married, know that God is still transforming you. Truth be told, He is still transforming all of us. He shapes us like a potter shapes clay. He is preparing suitable mates for those singles who desire to be married. God said that Adam needed a companion that would be suitable, and He knew that Adam needed someone who would be compatible. The Word of God tells us to not be unequally yoked together, so that means we need to be with someone who is compatible and comparable. Where the two become one, and they grow to fit each other without losing their own individuality; they endure hardships and good times together.

"God has infinite attention to spare for each one of us. You are as much alone with him as if you were the only being he had ever created." - C.S. Lewis

Whenever I feel lonely and my world becomes overwhelming, I remind myself that God's presence is everywhere. He commands His attention and love to my miniature world and that of others simultaneously. God is omnipresent. He can do more in a minute than I can do in years. I've learned to take a deep breath and place my entire trust in

Him, even when I feel as though he may not be as responsive to my prayers as I'd like Him to be.

He is attentive to our every need, wants, and longings as is a mother nursing her infant. When my daughter, Charlie, was around five months old, there were times when she would just cry to get my attention, especially, if I seemed far away or if I was in another room and out of her sight. She would cry if she couldn't feel me, hear me, or see me. This is how we are toward God at times; when hopelessness embraces our senses, we cry out and seek the attention of God. But even when we don't hear him, see him, or feel him we must understand that He is still very near to us. The Bible says that it's in Him that we live, move and have our being. We are alive because He is near to us! I challenge you to draw closer to God and watch Him draw closer to you.

Solitary confinement in incarceration camps and prisons is sometimes used as a form of reprimanding, and researchers indicate that it can become harmful to your senses and alertness and potentially lead to suicide. One study even shows that solitary confinement can cause social atrophy. I believe that when we fail to firmly grab a hold of the presence of God in our deepest moments of isolation, we are left feeling hopeless. God is a present help in the time of trouble, and He is readily willing and able to restore what you have lost and to renew your hope. Past hurts can cause us to isolate from even those with good intentions. But we must learn to fully trust God and cast our cargo of problems onto Him, knowing that He is trustworthy, faithful, and cares for us. Put on the garment of praise instead of a spirit of despair. Many singles are experiencing loneliness and depression, and if you are encountering this, I encourage you to seek God for godly relationships and godly counsel. Talk to your pastors and pray that the Holy Spirit leads you to a haven of rest. Find a small group of singles who may share the same interest and obstacles you face to show you ways to flourish in the season of solitary.

"Those who know your name (Jesus) trust in you, for you, Lord, have never forsaken those who seek you." Psalm 9:10

8. Favor in the Field

"So shall you find favor, good understanding, and high esteem in the sight of God and man." -Luke 2:52

Favor is goodwill and approval towards a person or thing.

The Old Testament book of Ruth is about a faithful Moabite woman whose husband, brother-in-law and father-in-law all died, leaving her, Orpah (her sister-in-law) and Naomi (her mother-in-law) alone. Here we have three women who all faced a loss of the same nature, a loss that changed their lives forever and caused their faith to be tested. Three mourning widows who had to face the intense challenge of returning to singlehood, each grieved the loss of intimacy and the closeness of a spouse; no longer could they cuddle or hear the voice of that loved one. His presence was no longer felt and had become as escapable as the wind. How does anyone cope with a loss like this? After the deaths of her sons, Naomi persistently asked her daughter-in-law's to return to their own homelands because she had no other sons for them to marry. Orpah decided to return home, but Ruth committed to stay with Naomi, not realizing that favor would soon meet her in the field. Even amid their mourning, their actions predicated their future.

You may or may not have experienced the loss of a loved one to the clenches of the grave, instead, you may have had a terrible break-up or divorce. If so, what did your reactions toward it say about your faith? Did anguish move you toward bitterness?

I find it unique that these three women lost their husbands in a similar manner, yet, not one of them was isolated from sharing the other's ambiguity and agony of losing a spouse. What we can learn from these widows is that we can't allow our mourning to dictate our faith. They were all faced with what was now a paradigm shift in their lives. The men in those days were the breadwinners and protectors of their homes, so to instantly go from something safe to something shaky was traumatic. No longer could they wake up in the warm arms of their husbands. They had to come to terms with the instant discontinuation of affection and intimacy.

Mourning is okay and is a definite and necessary part of the healing process. Ecclesiastes 3 lets us know that there is "*a time to weep and a time to laugh, a time to mourn and a time to dance*," but it's important to not allow your mourning to triumph over your faith in God.

For Orpah, Ruth's sister-in-law, returning to her homeland was in her personal best interest, after-all, it was a place of familiarity and comfort, and would afford her the opportunity to cope with her new normal. It can be scary moving forward when you don't know what to expect and I'm sure Orpah hadn't planned to be single prematurely; she hadn't planned for this loss. It seemed to be an unexpected death, and this was not what Orpah had in mind. Her love story was not supposed to end like this. At his burial, she wept and wept because she hadn't planned for such an abrupt interruption to her life. She found herself resentful for leaping out on faith and serving the God of her husband's ancestors. Orpah decided to turn back to a familiar land leaving Ruth and Naomi to continue in their journey. Sometimes life can present unexpected interruptions and, because of disappointment or just a lack of understanding, we return to things that no longer serve a purpose, like familiar relationships, self-ambitious plans, and stagnant places that are no longer meaningful nor productive. These are very vulnerable moments when our faith is greatly tested. Galatians 6:9, *"Be not weary in well doing for in due season we will reap if we faint not."* Weariness causes us to wander from place to place seeking rest only to have it endlessly flee. I assure you that when you diligently seek God, you will find rest for your soul.

Make up your mind today that you will cast all your cares, anxieties, apprehensions, and distresses upon Him. Strive to take Jesus' yoke upon you because His yoke is easy, and His burden is light. There is nothing too difficult for God to do; He's able to redeem and deliver us from all strongholds of the enemy, so begin to declare that all your irrational thoughts, ideas, and habits must remain under the subjection and authority of Jesus Christ. And a practical thing to do is, learn to find the good in each day and write it down in a private journal. For many, this has proven to be therapeutic.

I believe that if Orpah had made up her mind that returning to poverty, ineffective rituals, redundancy without results, self-hate and fear was not an option, she would have found favor in her field. Returning to accustomed seasons will only restrict us to fear and prohibit us from active faith. Even when you experience fear, move in faith, knowing that God has not given us a spirit of fear, but of love, power, and a sound mind. We need the power of God to withstand the trials ahead, the love of God to remain optimistic, and a sound mind guarded by reasonable understanding.

Once Orpah decided to leave Naomi and return to familiarity, the story of her faith stopped; nothing else about her life is recorded. I believe that Orpah's return home caused her to miss out on God's best intended end. Don't allow grief or disappointment to cause you to go backwards. What you left behind is withered and no longer brings about elevation, so, realize that whatever thing is no longer present can no longer produce. In order for the branch to produce fruit, it must be attached to the vine. Our vine is Jesus Christ and we must be attached to Him and remain in Him to see the full manifestation of His glory in our lives, regardless of who left you or the rejection you've endured. Stay the course and remain in His favor while in the field, *"So will you find favor, good understanding, and high esteem in the sight of God and man."* (Proverbs 3:4).

After Naomi lost her husband and two sons, she joined herself to shame and relished in the blame game; she mourned and afterwards criticized God's favor on her life. Honestly, sometimes the emotional effects of trials and losses can be discouraging. The loss or removal of a loved one is a life changing event; however, God will not put more on us than we can bear at any given moment, and if you feel like He does, then you just may be stronger than you think. God knows how much we can take. Although at times, the darkening shadow of mourning hangs over us like a cloud, the favor of God remains. Praise and thank Him amid trying times. Why? Because, God can make the end of your life far better than the beginning. Naomi mourned greatly, to the point where she isolated herself from her close-knit relationships with both of her daughter-in-law's. She exemplified how depression and pain can push people away and cause you to segregate yourself and shut out those who love you. It's important that we are intentional about how we conduct ourselves in delicate moments, and choose proper coping mechanisms when mourning because, if we're not careful, we can make the mistake of even shutting God out, and He's the one we need most.

Despite all, God had compassion towards Naomi because His ultimate goal was to bless her greatly, and He did it through the obedience of Ruth the Moabite.

"Obedience to God is like fuel in a car. The more obedience to God you have, the further you'll go." - Vasha Tolbert

In spite of Ruth's hurt, rejection, and pain, she connected to Naomi and had a deep love, appreciation, and adoration for her. Ruth didn't realize that Naomi would be the very person God would use to mentor her into the next part of her life. Orpah left, but Ruth connected. Even when famine hit their land, Ruth persevered. The famine caused Naomi and Ruth to later travel and seek a place of better opportunities for well- being. God's love can be quite comical, can't it? He loved Ruth and Naomi, and favored them, but His favor led them into famine – a drought; a recession, an economy on the decline, yet that wasn't the end of His plan. Have you ever felt like God's love led you into famine or a drought?

Naomi was moving forward to a land of the unknown, so Ruth's choosing to remain with Naomi forced her to cut ties with Orpah. Ruth had to decide which relationship she wished to remain connected to. Naomi was moving forward and Orpah was returning home. At times, we may be engulfed with the challenge to move forward or turn back. Ruth cared about both Orpah and Naomi and, like us, she was faced with a life-altering proposition. Sometimes God will give you an ultimatum to choose one or the other, your past or your future, your abundance or your lack, the person He is calling you to be or the person you have always been. Ruth would possibly never see Orpah again, but she had to mature in her purpose and calling and be willing to lose friendships that no longer served purpose in order to get all that God had for her. Ruth would not have had the opportunity to meet Boaz had she returned with Orpah and forsaken her mentor, Naomi. This reassures us that our best days in Christ are always ahead and never behind, and that God is eternally blessing us and making our crooked paths straight. He is a lamp unto our feet and a light unto our paths. It delights my spirit to know that God blesses us even in unfamiliar places. When God orchestrates a covenant, He does it with a mission in mind.

When Ruth's husband died, she wept, she mourned, she

grieved, but she pressed forward, and found favor in the field where she met a man of God named Boaz.

Marriage is more than taking selfies with matching colors and posting hashtag relationship goals on social media; it's a covenant between two partners. A covenant is more than doing household chores and bathing the children; it goes beyond the number of karats in a wedding ring and the saving of the wedding cake topper. Marriage is a mission and when God orchestrates a kingdom covenant, He does it with a mission in mind. I believe that God ordains husbands and wives as soul mates, like Adam and Eve, Mary and Joseph, Esther and King Ahasuerus, Christ and His Church, Ruth and Boaz; all of these biblical marriages were tied to missions. I also believe it grieves the heart of God when we choose to marry individuals who are not a part of our God-assigned mission. Marriage is more than quenching sexual passions. It's about excelling ministry and furthering the kingdom of God together. For this reason, Ecclesiastes 4:9-10 says that *"Two are better than one, because they have a good reward for their labor. For if they fall, the one will lift up his fellow: but woe to him that is alone when he falleth; for he hath not another to help him up.*" One can cover the other when chaos arises. Marriage is an agreement, so how can you marry someone who is not in agreement with God? It is better to wait for your mission partner than settle for a partner of misery.

Years ago, I was in a public restroom at work and there was a young lady on her cell phone abrasively yelling at what must have been her boyfriend. I mean, she was completely livid and in utter disagreement with him altogether. Sis, was fed up! The fact that she was yelling in a public facility in front of people, proved that she cared less if anyone heard her. I felt bad for her because every woman should feel appreciated and loved. This woman's call opened my eyes and caused me to really recognize that God did not design relationships to be agonizing, or humiliating, and He certainly didn't design marriage for misery. This is why you can't entertain anything or anyone that constantly brings pain. So, you aren't going on a rampage setting cars on fire in a parking lot somewhere, sis. It takes faith to accept love and reject lust. If you are struggling with letting go of what is weighing you down, I pray that God grants you the strength to walk away from toxic and unfruitful relationships. It is far better and sometimes easier to walk away early than to run away later. Value your time and guard your heart from anything or anyone sent to set you off course. There have been many times while dating that the Holy Spirit has revealed to me signs that a man was not for me. When these signs showed up, I simply redeemed my time and refrained from wasting any more time with that individual. Time is valuable and irreplaceable, so who we choose to invest our time with is crucial. Redeem your time. You are not obligated to sow seeds in bad soil.

Connect to God and His Spirit will lead you to your favored field.

Many singles rush into marriage with little to no

committed goals for it; no talks are had about the impact the marriage will contribute to their local communities and/or the world. What usually ends up happening is, the marriage perishes because there was never a vision established for it. Just like we saw the hand of God work in Ruth's life, we must become aware of the presence of God in our very own season of singleness. Your foundation is being solidly built and firmly established for the God-ordained spouse that sooner or later will be introduced into the picture. God is laying concrete upon concrete, stone upon stone, and aligning corner to corner. He is getting you all the way together!

Isaiah 28:16 (NKJV) *"Therefore thus says the Lord God: "Behold, I lay in Zion a stone for a foundation, A tried stone, a precious cornerstone, a sure foundation; Whoever believes will not act hastily."*

I had to learn to not hate the wait, and by that, I mean enjoy waiting on God's perfect timing. Please understand that your waiting is working for you, just like it has and still is working for me, so, there is no need to act hastily or quickly marry without first considering the field. Vetting your mate and praying to God and waiting for confirmation and clarity is vital to the longevity of a relationship. Trust and believe that God is molding, shaping, and sharpening for you a sure, steady, and a solid foundation that cannot be easily removed by tribulation or persecution that marriages often face. I'd rather wait to marry right than hate the wait and marry wrong. Let's intentionally decide to wait right. How can you wait right? By yielding your self-will over to God. Say a simple but earnest prayer, "*Lord, I do not feel like waiting today, but despite my feelings and my mood I will wait on you. I desire to wait right, not by my will or my way, but by Your will, way and in your timing.*" God's way and will is always right and perfectly timed. Orpah hated the wait, which caused her to turn to her former land and miss what may have been her best years just ahead. You see, Ruth waited right. Allow the wait to work; be assured, it's working for you – all you gotta' do is let it work!

Ruth was an honorable example of trusting God in her

wait; not only that, but she waited the right way. You may ask, "How can I wait right?" That is a fair question, so let's dissect it a bit more. Ruth 2:2 (NKJV) *"So Ruth the Moabitess said to Naomi, "Please let me go to the field, and glean heads of grain after him in whose sight I may find favor." And she said to her, "Go, my daughter."*

When Ruth went into the field, that was God sending His favor into the field. You see, you are the favor of God. Proverbs 18:22 (NKJV) says, *"He who finds a wife finds a good thing and obtains favor from the Lord."* Girl, you are favor that must be found! But you must first be willing to go out into the field. What good man in his right mind finds treasure and then throws it in the ocean to be forgotten? None! When Jesus returns, He is coming to take His bride, the church. This is the revealing ideology of a divinely appointed marriage. The man who finds a wife finds favor of the Lord; he then acquires this newly found favor and takes it for himself. How can favor be found if not in the field? I'm sure you are reading the term *field* thinking of a barn of hay and wild trotting animals. Yes, that can be the setting of a field, but so can a school campus, community center, grocery store, workplace, library, church, and so on and so forth. The field can be communicated as God's Positioning System (GPS). In order to be found, you must be in position. Many single women think they are to find the man, but God did not create women to hunt for a spouse; He created men with the gift of pursuing and women with the gift of intuition. Women were designed to be placed in position to be found, and to utilize their gifted ability to select a solid prospect by perception and not deception. Listen to your intuition to combat deception, and if your gut is telling you something is off, you may very well be right. Position yourself properly and remember, you are the favor of the Lord. Just as God positioned Ruth to be found, He is positioning you too.

Select by perception and not deception!

I had the pleasure of leading a singles ministry called Singles Selected to Serve, and one of the things we often discussed was the importance of developing yourself, serving God, and working your field. My personal

experience is this: years ago, I dimmed in faith and stopped believing God to do anything favorable or admirable when it came down to dating. Dating was difficult for me. There were times when the thought of having to get to know someone was exhausting. I hated having to be vulnerable with a stranger. And having to transition into a CIA Agent to ensure the brother wasn't lyin', okay? Don't judge me! It's called research, okay?

I dated off and on and managed to abstain from having sex. I'll be frank and say that it was easy to not have sex when there was no interest, or I barely found the man attractive, but it was hard to resist when I did find them enjoyable to look at and especially if chemistry was present. Now, I will confess I have made out, and I'm talking sloppy kissing and heavy panting making out. There were times, I had to walk away before it went too far. Talk about a strong love for Jesus! After experiencing one failed relationship after another, I no longer had a desire to date. I was frustrated and didn't care to go out to the movies with a group of friends or bowling or anything of that nature. I had become comfortable in my everyday routine of going to work and coming back home. My shrunken faith had distanced me from the field, but the Holy Spirit convicted me. Overtime I learned that God already favors me; He favors me *where* I am and *how* I am. It was time to break out of my fear of hoping again, and it was time to work my field, so I intentionally began making plans to truly enjoy the season of singleness on purpose.

Love the you that you are today. Don't hate today, aiming to love tomorrow. Love today, enjoy where you are in this moment. Hebrews 11:6 says, "*And without faith it is* impossible to please God", and it also says in Matthew 11:12 "And from the days of John the Baptist until now the kingdom of heaven suffereth violence, and the violent take it by force." We must vehemently work the principles of God consistently to see results in our lives. Applying these two passages of Scripture to my life opened quite a few doors that I am still gaining from today. Just being thankful to God for the small things led me to see the bigger things. The Bible tells us to acknowledge God in all our ways and He will direct our paths (Proverbs 3:6). Acknowledgment is the gatekeeper to elevation. In this season of singleness, I have learned to use my faith to agree with God's heavenly and eternal plans for my life. I admonish you to get out of your box, even if that means talking yourself into going to places you have never explored. God wants to do a new thing in your life. You can become successfully single! I vowed to no longer spend my life pitying being single, and, because of my intentional endeavor to explore the field, I have advanced in self-confidence and God-confidence. I can be great! We are children of God, no matter our marital status, so, we must remember that God will be whatever we need Him to be, whenever we need Him to be it. The gaps in your life, don't worry, He is a gap-filler. He will never leave nor forsake you even in your times of feeling unwanted, deprived, and heartbroken. He is right there with you.

I often tell myself that God favors me too much to share me too soon with just anyone. Trust His timing! I constantly joke about how heaven is without clocks. You see, I live in Florida where our time zone is three hours ahead of California; we share the same eastern standard time zone as New York, but, I've come to realize that our time zones are not beyond God's control. My impatience has taught me to trust the timing of God. Our clocks do not have authority, power, and dominion over God's strategic timing. God does not orchestrate on eastern, pacific nor central standard time. Quite the opposite in fact - He operates on eternal, supernatural time. He is the beginning and the ending of time. God is the hand keeping our clocks ticking. We wouldn't be able to function on eastern standard time if it weren't for His eternal, supernatural time. Gosh, it makes me feel a lot better, knowing that I cannot be as self-centered as I sometimes try to be. I used to cry and cry for companionship, always thinking how ideal it would be to have a man present to do three things for me: (1) pay and sponsor my needs and wants,

(2) to have great-amazing sex, and (3) to have someone to listen to me talk his ear off at the end of each work day.

Extra help with the bills, great sex, and a good head nod every now and then, while I ramble on about my opinions and ideas, would make my life great from time to time, but, I don't have either of those things yet, and guess what - life is still great.

I am still elevating. I am actively pursuing my bachelor's in legal studies, I am making more money than I have ever made in my life, and I have a supportive family who loves me. And, do you want to know the best and most freeing thing about it all? My daughter, Charlie gets to see me (her mother) charge through barriers. She watches me break glass ceilings without the accompaniment of a spouse. Charlie gets to see that women are a force to be reckoned with and that we can achieve whatever we put our minds to. My daughter will grow up with the understanding that women can live a life full of passion, purpose, and precedence. I don't consider myself a feminist, but I do believe that God uses whomever He wills, and He will use a woman - spoiler alert. In a misogynistic world, women are actively becoming trailblazers. Women around the world are setting the tone on what it looks like to elevate without a mate. I know that women are the favor of God – no doubt! I believe favor is simply the anointing of God. In modern day era, we tend to seek fiction (false realities) and not favor. If we are not careful, we will find ourselves seeking drama instead of destiny. Fiction is considered anything outside of a realistic expectation. I struggled with this a lot while dating. My expectations of the person I chose to date was unbelievably unrealistic, and honestly for no real reason. I set false expectations on myself and others and began forecasting my insecurities onto my loved ones. I don't know why I did it; maybe it was to keep from allowing anyone into my heart. I didn't want to be vulnerable and I didn't want to get hurt, so, I raised my walls and made them metal. I stopped everyone at the gate! It looked something like this: If they didn't serve me, my needs, my wants, my vision, then they were not the one. But, the better way of looking at dating would be, how has God called me to serve this individual in this season of my life? These are two different approaches to rationalizing your expectations. Even Jesus came to serve and not be served, and, I believe if we are going to conduct ourselves in the light of God, we must be willing to first ask Him, how best can we serve. The Bible says, it is better to give than to receive. Realistic expectations are necessary, and there is a difference between earnest expectations and fictitious expectations. God is not concerned with blessing you so you can look blessed but blessing you so you can be blessed.

Years ago, I vividly remember driving a raggedy 1987 Grand Marquis; it was decent for a while, but eventually began to have so many troubles until it forced me into car shopping. Y'all, the car was so raggedy! It had served its purpose, but I knew it was time for a greater blessing from God. I felt in my heart that God was going to bless me very well because I was faithful in ministry, I had remained holy as best I could before Him and I was confident that all the hard work I'd invested certainly would not go unnoticed. The AC eventually stopped working in the car, and one day Charlie complained about the inside of the car being hot; only two of the windows would go down at this point. My bright idea was to just speed up to get more breeze, praying to God that I wouldn't get a speeding ticket. On top of that, the key got stuck in the ignition! I went to remove the key from the ignition one day, and it just would not come out, so I left it. Because the key was stuck in the ignition, I couldn't lock the doors when I got out of the car. Y'all, the car was falling apart piece by piece. I couldn't afford to replace the ignition. So being the resourceful person that I am, I took a scarf and tied it around the steering wheel to hide the key stuck in the ignition, so no one steals my car. You see, when you have been single for some time, you become somewhat innovative another perk to singleness! I cannot express how desperately my daughter, Charlie, and I needed another car. I once locked myself out the car and had to break in publicly to get inside – talk about embarrassment! I was so over it.

As a result, I went car shopping with a lot of faith and a little money, and at the time I wanted a white Range Rover. For months I searched for this white Range Rover, regardless of my little finances, and finally found it at a car lot in Fort Lauderdale. It was as beautiful as I'd expected, but there was already 100,000 miles on the engine. The monthly payments would have wiped me clean; the vehicle was more than ten years old and the down payment was much more than I'd anticipated. Disappointed and left with my unmet and false expectations, I left the Range Rover at the car lot and drove back home in my 87' Grand Marquis. Needless to say, it was a pretty slow and quiet ride home. To add insult to injury, it rained heavily on the way back to Fort Myers. Oh, I forgot to add, my windshield wipers no longer worked because the fuse had blown. Thankfully, we made it home safely. A few months later, my car began to smoke while I was driving to work, and, at this point, I was completely at my wits end. With tears in my eyes, I prayed, "God you promised to take care of us. What are we going to do without a car?" It wasn't until I sought God for an answer that He revealed that my expectations were far from realistic and from what He wanted to do in my life at the time. In that moment, I understood that the Range Rover was considered a false expectation because it was outside of the will of God for my life. Sometimes, when we pray to God, we don't seek His will, instead, we tell Him our will and ask Him to make it happen. I could have very well purchased the Range Rover, but it didn't make sense, and I knew it would not have been a smart choice. Had I purchased the Range Rover like I wanted, who knows how much of a financial burden I would have created for myself. With the car already having 100,000 miles, who knows if the car would still be operable today.

Within the same month, God blessed me with a much newer car that had only 30,000 miles on it. God blessed me with a 2014 vehicle in 2015. It worked great and was much more affordable. It was perfect, and believe it or not, was not my original desire. Throughout all this God truly taught me to be realistic and to ignore false realities.

The Bible declares that God will give us the desires of our hearts if we delight ourselves in Him, so I challenge you to delight yourself in God. The most important part of truly delighting ourselves in Him is our priorities change. The attitude of getting what you want right now will change as you elevate. You begin to value God for who He is, not just for what He can give to you. I think when you reach this special place in your life, you are better positioned to receive your heart's desires. Do you know that God will often change your desires? Have you ever wanted something so badly only to get it and realize you didn't really want it, you just thought you did? You probably just liked the thought of having it. Well, I have.

As a matter of fact, that was me with the Range Rover. There were times where I dated men who I wanted to be with only to date them and find out, we wanted different things in life and working towards a relationship would be unsalvageable. Allow God to renew your desires, because oftentimes we can desperately want something not realizing that God has something far better in store. What God has for you may even exceed your expectation, and when you get it, you will think to yourself, "Wow, this is much better than what I had in mind." He wants you to desire what He desires for you. How funny is it to think that when we delight ourselves in God, He begins to change our hearts, and our changed hearts produce idyllic wants? I didn't think I could love a car that I hadn't been searching for, but when I submitted my will to God and became willing to accept what He knew was best for me, my desire changed. The thing I wanted changed. I became receptive to newness. And I want to encourage you to acquire a taste for God's presence, and once you do that, you are in for a ride of a lifetime.

It is a good thing to have an earnest expectation, in fact, the Bible encourages us to wait for the coming of the Lord with an earnest expectation (Luke 12:40), but experience has taught me to earnestly desire God's best for me. You see, the Range Rover was my best but came with several issues, however, my new car was His best for me, and it worked perfectly. God's best cooperates with our destiny.

Here is another fictitious expectation: Most of the people I see throughout my workday despise their jobs and find it difficult to enjoy Monday through Thursday. Nearly every weekday when asked how their day is going, the redundant response is, "Well, it's almost Friday!" These words cause me dismay because there are people who only find life enjoyable on Fridays, and God doesn't want us to live our lives that way. Wasting precious time waiting for

Friday to arrive is a false reality, because every waking moment of each day is an opportunity to elevate. The word of God encourages us to be content in every season. This includes our days of singleness. Even in marriage it is important to be content. Philippians 4:11 (KJV) – *"Not that I speak in respect of want: for I have learned, in whatsoever state I am, therewith to be content."* Why is deciding to be content imperative? It's because contentment is a state of peace and tranquility and learning to be content avoids irrational decision making. Every day may not be a good day, but you can find the good in every day. I personally choose to enjoy each day, be purposeful, and bring joy to everyone I encounter. Again, I cannot say every day will be sunny side up, but I can say that favor cannot be produced out of anything fictitious, cynical, or negative. If we want or need anything from God, we may as well work on our attitudes and expectations long before He gives it to us. Get ready beforehand and adjust your attitude now!

Just the other day someone made me so mad, I wanted

to throw a vase at a wall. Don't call the cops, I didn't follow through with it. It was just a thought. And, yes, I did repent. When I feel myself near to tipping my drink over in frustration, I must remind myself that everything I desire to see must first begin in me. Would I want God to bless me with a husband who would need to endure my ruthless temper and unstable behavior? Absolutely not! How can I be a blessing to others in my life with an ungrateful and complaining demeanor? If I made everyone miserable around me, at my workplace, the company's turn-over rate would be ridiculously high because of my sour-puss attitude, or I'd eventually be fired. I believe in order to reach full spiritual maturity; God must be able to trust you with His favor. The Bible tells us that *Jesus grew in wisdom and stature, and in favor with God and man* (Luke 2:52). This depiction of Jesus is God's desire for us all, that we grow into His favor. Did you know favor just means that you are a likable person? It concerns me when Christians are unable to work well with others. The Apostle Paul encourages us to get along with all men if possible. Can you imagine if Ruth bickered with Boaz's workers while trying to glean in the field? What would her end have looked like had she gossiped about the other workers or became a negative Nancy? How can you glean and be mean? I'm almost certain the field manager would have had someone escort Ruth off the property and she would have forfeited her favor with Boaz. Who knows how God would have had to step in to rectify that situation? God has not released favor to many singles because of misdirected attitudes and cynical perspectives during the waiting process. I am thankful that Ruth kept a good attitude and was able to work well with others while waiting. Not long ago, I took an interest in a gentleman at work; he was kind, funny, and very handsome.

Periodically we would see each other and speak in passing, but, after a while, I began to grow a keen interest in him. I was uncertain if he wished to get to know me on a more personal level, but I was eager to find out. I figured what the heck; if I approach him, what's the worst that could happen, after all, I had been out of the dating game a long time. So, I purchased a 'Hello' card and wrote a nice little note inside which read: "Hello, I think you are kind, funny, and handsome. I will be out of town this week for a conference, but I am open to hanging out if you would like to." (I included my personal cell and signature). I put the note in an envelope and the note was placed on the windshield of his car. Regrettably, the gentleman never called. While at the conference in Orlando, I sporadically questioned what might happen when I returned to work. At one point I thought, *"Yep, he called the cops; I shouldn't have written the note. After all, who still handwrites notes in the 21st century, Vasha? Woman, is you crazy! You are asking to make the headlines of the newspapers. He now thinks that I am a stalker and I will for sure be on our 6 o'clock news channel. Way to go, Vasha!"* After several days with no call or text, I truly did not look forward to my return to work. The morning of my return, he waited for me in the parking lot, where we usually said hello and crossed each other in passing. He confirmed receiving the note and went on to explain that the reason he did not contact me was because he was currently seeing a woman whom he liked a lot and, out of respect to her, he decided not to reach out to me. He said he was flattered by the note and hoped to continue seeing me around, and we continued to casually discuss the conference I had attended. Although the outcome was not what I expected, I remained cordial and trusted that I had the favor of God on my life, still. I am learning that it takes faith to date, glean in the field, and open yourself up to others without a guaranteed favorable outcome, along with potentially receiving rejection. My co-worker jokingly advised that I could always follow up with an 'Apology' note to counteract the failed 'Hello' note. Let me be clear, I have no intentions of following up with an apology note because I certainly don't want to risk catching a harassment charge. At the least it brought a smile to the gentleman's face.

Faith to Date

It takes courage to date and position yourself to be favored. Ruth was not only faithful, but she was courageous and persevered. She kept her focus on her family, Naomi. She strategized to maximize her gifts in her season of singleness. Before Ruth's decision to go to the field, she walked in humility and sought godly counsel from Naomi regarding whether she should access the field for provision. It's important and rewarding to seek direction from God, and it is advisable to use the godly relationships surrounding you. Proverbs 11:14 says, *"Where there is no counsel, the people fall; But in the multitude of counselors there is safety."* There are good relationships and godly relationships, in the which I will discuss the difference between goodly and godly relationships later. Ruth had been faithful to care for Naomi and their relationship grew as deep as mother and daughter, because the two honored each other as such. Naomi was a voice of reasoning in the life of Ruth. Years had passed since her husband died, but she remained hopeful. Ruth had enough faith to glean, and she expected favor despite her circumstances. Faithfulness is an artifact of favor. In Ruth's faithfulness to her mother-in-law, Naomi, she found favor in the sight of God and man - she found favor in the site of Boaz. Regardless of past circumstances and imperfections, God wants us to remain faithful to Him. Even amid uncertainty, remain persistent.

Dating is nothing more than strategizing. How? Because each party comes to the table with conditions, standards, and expectations. So, knowing this tad-bit of information should cause us, to better improve our dating tactics and position ourselves to be led to glean in the field of opportunity.

How do you attain the favor of God? By persisting in faithfulness, delighting in the things of God, and allowing Him to properly position you. Ruth, by God's divine providence, was strategically positioned in Boaz's field. As we consider this, it should make us a little more cognizant of God's subtle way of maneuvering us exactly where we need to be when we need to be there. This is what happens when we stumble into success. Glance back over your life and you will find that many of the blessings you've obtained you just stumbled upon. Likewise, this is the case for me, also. Ruth 2:3 (NKN) *"Then she left and went and gleaned in the field after the reapers. And she happened to come to the part of the field belonging to Boaz, who was of the family of Elimelech."* In a season of solitary (singleness), God teaches us that in order to embrace His favor, we have to abandon the familiar. In this passage, Ruth knew that it would be best to go to the field for provision, and she understood her need to step away from that which was familiar, comfortable, and common to her. At some point, we may all experience a familiar field. That familiar field may be a past relationship, an addiction, toxic friendships, insecurities, and so forth. A favored field and a familiar field may not be too far from each other; possibly within walking distance, however, they both produce totally different outcomes. A favored field produces good fruit and prosperity. A familiar field produces nothing short of weeds, worms, lack, and deterioration. We have the choice of gleaning in a familiar field or stepping out into the favored field God has prepared for us. It takes faith to experience the favored field because it requires faith to wait and faith to date. Several years ago, I worked for a technical support company and had been employed with them for a little over four years. A part of the interview process required me to complete a computer assessment test to confirm my knowledge of electronics, and honestly, I only knew the basics, like how to turn the television on and off, change the channels, and roam through the guide to see what was showing. And, as far as computers, I knew how to turn them on and off, how to use the Internet, and how to save files and pictures. That was it! Before I applied to this company, I worked as a home health-aid, caring for the elderly-disabled. My bi-weekly salary averaged about $300, so, I made a total of $600.00 a month. I was desperately struggling financially to take care of me and my daughter. Things had gotten so bad until I was sleeping on my mother's living room floor with my seven-month old daughter. But even while we snuggled on my mother's cold tile floor, God was supplying our every need.

When I didn't have the resources to even buy diapers, my friends would randomly supply them not even having a clue how much I needed them. Subtly, God was making a way. Eventually, I felt the need to transition. I have noticed during transitional phases of my life, that before my outer world could change, something had to first take place within me, meaning, in my spirit. I began to comprehend that God had something better for me and that through Jesus Christ, I could experience an abundant life. Before I got the new job, I researched the salary and began to calculate the total income possible (I do this before accepting any job offer). I would consider the field before transitioning or even knowing if I was considered a candidate. I knew that if I wanted the Kingdom life the Bible talked about, I would have to fight for it because it wouldn't be just handed to me. Like me, you too must fight for elevation. Just imagine all the obstacles you encounter along the way. Hard times will challenge your motive for wanting better. Over the span of time, God elevated me; He raised me up and exalted me. With each employer I've had, there has been increase financially, spiritually, and mentally. I have found that with every level comes new devils but new resources and opportunities. Just like video games, each time you are promoted to a higher level, you undergo greater attacks, but in each of them you learn new strategies and tactics. In some games, the reward is advanced machinery, cars, or more spending wages. Similarly, we undergo hardships and at times we are rewarded for doing well. It's up to us to level up! It's up to us to elevate! That's what Ruth did. She leveled up. She was determined to use her platform and favor to find grace in the field. If we could picture Ruth in today's era, we would see her as a hardworking, very strong-minded woman. She would resemble a single woman who was tenacious, grounded, and a trailblazer, because, she knew that someone else (in this case, Naomi) was depending on her strength and she would not disappoint her. We all have someone depending on us to make right decisions, and, believe it or not, the decisions we make today could affect the people in our lives tomorrow. If I walked into my workplace and decided, you know what, I have had enough and abruptly quit, my decision would have a definite effect on my daughter. Even though God has given us free will, we must remember that every decision will lead to a doorway, some good, some bad, so it is imperative to think things through before acting. If Ruth were alive today, her priorities would be aligned with household maintenance and striving to stay afloat of daily living expenses. There are many modern-day Ruth's - courageous women who make responsible decisions to provide for their homes; women who level up when the playing field seems unfair or when they are at a disadvantage, and women who pursue with purpose, deciding, against all odds, that it's never too late to win. These women are heroic. We see them! We know them! We are them!

When God led Ruth to find food in the field, she adorned herself to glean. My question to you is: Are you dressed to glean? Ruth was innovative and embodied intellect; she personified contentment, humility, and adaptability to every season she encountered. She dressed for the occasion and used her faith as a compass to know that no good deed goes unnoticed. Over the course of time, one of my most valuable lessons learned is to not lose my faith in God. For many of us, elevation doesn't just land on our front doorsteps, neither is it thrown in our laps. If we want it, we must go out and get it.

God has perfect timing, and although it may be challenging, we must learn to wait on it. James 1:17 (NIV) says, "Every good and perfect gift is from above, coming down from the Father of the heavenly lights, who does not change like shifting shadows." It's encouraging to know that His gifts are perfect and delivered to us through the HPS - Heavenly Postal Service. Corny- but true!

Boaz (Ruth's future husband) was a wealthy man who respected God, and one who admired Ruth's purity and loyalty. I believe the spouse God has in store for you will be astonished and flattered by your ability to stand alone and to stand tall. Confidence is a beautiful thing on a woman; it fits her curves better than a Dolce' & Gabanna dress. Confidence enables you to avoid compromising your values, beliefs, or standards. When Boaz saw that Ruth was fashioned in a different manner than the other maidservants, he inquired of her and found out that she was indeed a woman of loyalty and of prominence in the community, and he noted how she cared for her mother in law; this sparked an interest in him - he was hooked and infatuated! He heard that she was a good and godly woman with unchanging character, and this drew him to her. Singles, we must be cautious of the bait we use to draw a mate, because what you use to hook them is the bait you may need to keep them. God calls us a holy nation and peculiar people, and it's your peculiarity that attracts. The spouse God has for you will be drawn to your character and the God in you. Your God-ordained spouse will respect the God you serve. I have dated men who loved my shell (looks and physique) but despised the Spirit of God within me. The men I dated were handsome, but they couldn't entertain my membrane, so it caused me to get bored quickly. These types of connections are shallow and hold no value. I clearly understand now that God designed marriage so that both the husband and wife could reciprocate a love that grows from deep to deep.

I made up my mind to not tolerate or accept anything that comes into my life to pull me away from God. In the dating phase, much time is devoted to the other person, so, if that person disengages or interrupts the presence of God in your life, eventually you will need to decide whether to compromise your relationship with God to appease that person or let them go. We cannot serve God and narcissism at the same time; we will either love one or hate the other, but we cannot love and serve both.

9. Goodly and Godly People

It is time for parents to teach young people early on that in diversity there is beauty and there is strength. – Maya Angelou

(John 4:4-26 NIV) *Now he had to go through Samaria. So he came to a town in Samaria called Sychar, near the plot of ground Jacob had given to his son Joseph. Jacob's well was there, and Jesus, tired as he was from the journey, sat down by the well. It was about noon. When a Samaritan woman came to draw water, Jesus said to her, "Will you give me a drink?" {His disciples had gone into the town to buy food.) The Samaritan woman said to him, "You are a Jew and I am a Samaritan woman. How can you ask me for a drink?" For Jews do not associate with Samaritans. Jesus answered her, "If you knew the gift of God and who it is that asks you for a drink, you would have asked him, and he would have given you living water." "Sir," the woman said, "you have nothing to draw with and the well is deep. Where can you get this living water? Are you greater than our father Jacob, who gave us the well and drank* *from it himself, as did also his sons and his livestock?" Jesus answered, "Everyone who drinks this water will be thirsty again, but whoever drinks the water I give them will never thirst. Indeed, the water I give them will become in them a spring of water welling up to eternal life." The woman said to him, "Sir, give me this water so that I won't get thirsty and have to keep coming here to draw water." He told her, "Go, call your husband and come back." "I have no husband," she replied. Jesus said to her, "You are right when you say you have no husband. The fact is, you have had five husbands, and the man you now have is not your husband. What you have just said is quite true." Sir," the woman said, I can see that you are a prophet. Our ancestors worshiped on this mountain, but you Jews claim that the place where we must worship is in Jerusalem." Woman," Jesus replied, believe me, a time is coming when you will worship the Father neither on this mountain nor in Jerusalem. You Samaritans worship what you do not know; we worship what we do know, for salvation is from the Jews. Yet a time is coming and has now come when the true worshipers will worship the Father in the Spirit and in truth, for they are the kind of worshipers the Father seeks. God is spirit, and his worshipers must worship in the Spirit and in truth." The woman said, I know that Messiah" (called Christ) is coming. When he comes, he will explain everything to us." Then Jesus declared, I, the one speaking to you-I am he."*

I enjoy diversity and inclusion, so to sit at a table with people from various walks of life and to discover their way of thinking is always a unique opportunity. Being challenged to respect, listen, and respond to other's opinions is a life tool that, I think, we oftentimes miss. In 2018, I met a young, beautiful, and liberated Cuban woman. We will call her Carolyn. Immediately, we clicked, and it was quite funny because we were almost completely opposite in our thinking, upbringing, lifestyles, goals and so on. Here I was, a teacher of the Word of God while Carolyn frequently visited sports bars.

If someone crossed her the wrong way, she was going to let them have it on the spot. She had no limits and had little restraint in maintaining or even caring what others thought of her. She could care less about being the outcast at social events and many, if not most, of our coworkers chose not to socialize with her. To some, she came off as abrasive and intolerant, and most considered even hanging out with her as crossing the boundaries of their social acceptance. Carolyn enjoyed sex and ranted openly about her sex life with men she had met at the bar Friday night or a re-ignited fling of the past, and she cussed like a sailor skunk drunk on a Friday night. Her sexual engagements turned several of the uppity women off from her, but I liked Carolyn. I knew right away that she was not one that professed godliness and her religious beliefs greatly differed from mine. She'd always verbally admire my peaceful spirit and way of dealing with pressure. Carolyn and I laughed together a lot, and we both had a sense of humor that always kept the mood light and playful. One day, Carolyn asked me to hang out with her and another colleague after work; I paused a little and responded with, "let *me check my schedule.*" After finding a sitter for Charlie, I told Carolyn I accepted her invitation to unwind at the sports bar after work with her and a few of the girls. I wasn't sure what the night would hold, but I kept an open mind. Now, all my colleagues attending that night knew that I was a woman of faith and that I did not drink or smoke, but I loved good food and a good time. Shortly after work, I went home, got ready for the occasion, and headed to Millers Ale House. When I got there, the girls were all sitting on the outside patio, the music was cranked, and everyone was yelling over the music trying to carry on their conversations. Now, I had eaten at Millers Ale House plenty of times before but always sat inside of the restaurant area, never outside, so I quickly learned that the scenery and crowd was much different from indoors. The TV's played loudly broadcasting the current football and basketball games and the music blasted through the speakers on the patio. People were smoking, drinking, and the crowd was rowdy.

When the waiter greeted us, I ordered my usual, rice pilaf, steamed broccoli, grilled shrimp, and steak with a cup of water and lemon to drink. I had heard that Carolyn and the other women would go home with men from the bar, and that they spoke to strangers confidently and impulsively. But, for me, even looking at a guy felt awkward; I had been single for so long until flirting became bizarre. Flirting was awkward for me. I stopped noticing attention from men, minded my own business and if a gentleman spoke, I would speak back, but nothing out of the norm or no intent to pursue. I will admit I felt a bit outside my comfort zone hanging at a sports bar with women who, were openly promiscuous. Knowing this, I chose to keep an open mind and to remain true to my values and beliefs. Even at a sports bar hanging out at night, I believed in Jesus and knew, more than anything, that I wanted these women to know that they were loved for who they were. Even if the men they engaged with did not exemplify that love, I wanted to extend it through friendship. They ordered drink after drink to keep their buzz afloat, but I committed to my water with lemon. When they toasted in celebration with the dinging of glasses, I engaged with my glass of water with lemon. I enjoyed them and surprisingly they enjoyed me. Carolyn and I had great times together and still do; we laughed hysterically the entire time we were together. She often sought advice for personal things she'd go through with men. Our friendship was unique, unorthodox, and respectful because we respected each other's differences. Many women on my job disapproved of our hanging together because they felt she would somehow contaminate me, but I knew better. I also knew how some women could make others, who were outcasts, feel terrible about themselves. I didn't heed their advice, because I knew who I was in God, and to isolate others because we differed in thoughts, ways or lifestyles wasn't the right thing to do. So, I determined to be above the women who shunned Carolyn because she was wild and promiscuous. I chose to love her despite her lifestyle and to offer my friendship, and I am grateful to God that she accepted. I think it is more important than ever to break away from the divide and conquer approach we have taken to maintain our social reputations and stigmas. We have become people who are more concerned with personal prominence than we are with just loving people. We mistakenly place our politics over the best interest of others who vary from us in cultural differences, ethnic makeup, economical class, and diversity of thought. Putting your ambitions before people was not the philosophy Jesus demonstrated through his life here on earth. In fact, Jesus valued the outcasts. In John 4, He went out of His way to meet a woman of Samaria, and throughout the Bible, a lot of people who were desperate for deliverance, healing, and destiny ran after Jesus. This Samaritan woman was sought eagerly by Jesus. Why would Jesus go out of His way to meet an unstable whore who appeared worthless to an entire nation? Because, Jesus loves an outcast who is authentic and has a good heart. That is why.

According to Time Article (https://time.com/5609124/-ussuicide-rate-increase/), "As of 2017, the male suicide rate was more than three times higher than the female rate. But female suicide rates are rising more quickly—by 53% since 1999, compared to 26% for men—and the gap is narrowing." Realizing the rising suicide rates of both males and females, should provide us a sense of urgency in making others feel welcomed. We should be encouraged to be the ones that Jesus will use to exemplify love to everyone and most importantly to those who are seemingly unloved. Remember, Jesus sat with sinners; He tolerated those whose habits opposed His and whose thoughts, walks and talks contrasted His own. God doesn't love godly people more than He loves good people; we are all loved by Him. I have made it a habit to go out of my way to speak to the loners and women who are downtrodden. I believe that being the hands and feet of Jesus is necessary if we want to see suicide rates decrease. I lost my father at twelve years old to homicide, so I grew up with the understanding that life is valuable, and that tomorrow is not promised. That's the reason I strive to be peaceable with all men and women. I defuse quarrels and troublemakers and do my part to stand up for the defenseless and voiceless, not condoning bullying of any kind. What if we did our part to make sure that everyone we met, regardless of our differences, and marital status, felt the love of Christ through us? What if we made the commitment to love anyhow?

Knowing Carolyn has taught me to be more open-minded and not take myself so serious and I'm certain that Carolyn has come to admire many great things about me, as well. Although Carolyn is not godly, I consider her to be a good person, and I believe we all have good people in our lives. When Carolyn and I met, she was dealing with trauma from previous relationships therefore, she found it challenging to commit to a monogamous relationship, however, within a year, she met a man who adores her and her beautiful children, so she is now in a loving relationship and is very happy. She doesn't hang out as often as she did before because she enjoys spending time with her family. I usually invite my friends to church, and, although I would love for Carolyn to visit my church, I've decided to never ask her to visit. After much prayer and consideration, I believe that God has started a good work in her life eventhough she may not ever step foot in a church. The love that is extended to her through my friendship has at least opened her mind to know that there are godly people who enjoy just some good ole' folks. I hope that Carolyn knows that there are godly people

who honor God by living their lives according to His word,

who love her just like she is, and with no ulterior motives.

There are good people and there are godly people and we

need both types of relationships to keep us humble, prayerful,

and to bring balance. What makes a good person good? A

good person is someone who has a good heart. They may not

be considered churchy or fit in with most faith-based crowds,

but God still loves them. I believe good people are real people

who have made mistakes and are probably still making

mistakes. Goodly relationships offer balance. They teach you

to constantly extend grace for others who may not have a

relationship with Christ. Humility causes you to not condemn,

but extend grace, love, and oftentimes truth. When we fight to

love past the faults of someone else, we can learn how patient

God is with us.

Then there are the godly people who profess Jesus Christ

as the Son of God and who accept Jesus as their personal

Savior. They look like church folk, wearing the great big sun hats and dressing somewhat modestly. Although godly people are faithful to the Lord and His word, they make mistakes along the way just like good people. The difference between godly people and good people, is that when godly people make mistakes, they ask God for forgiveness and believe in their hearts that they have been forgiven. The contrast between the two can be subtle to great. I am empowered by godly relationships to continue in the faith and have gained a great deal of biblical principles and ways to apply them to my life. These godly relationships electrify and unify my goals. I have learned a lot from both goodly and godly people; they have all aided in my elevation without a mate.

An excerpt from the book Mud and the Masterpiece by John Burke reads as an activity on Chapter 1 page 36, *Jesus was a friend of sinners. He saw them in the identity God created them to live out. Our problem is too often we see what they are right now – the mud instead of the Masterpiece. To be like Jesus we need a new way of seeing others. The goal of this exercise is to intentionally open your heart to those you see muddied, and to learn their story in order to discover the Masterpiece God wants to restore. If you're a natural conversationalist, you may find this easy. If you're not, you can still have great conversations, you'll just need to stretch yourself. The Holy Spirit will give you the ability and courage if you are willing.*

I want to ask, "Are you willing?" You see, the women who tried to ostracize Carolyn didn't know her story and they didn't care to get to know it because they'd already written her off as a lost cause. When I began building my personal relationship with Jesus Christ, worship wasn't a part of my walk at all. I didn't grow up in church, as a matter of fact, when I was younger, I despised going to church. It made no sense to me why people would waste countless hours listening to someone talk about something and someone no one had ever seen. I figured there were much better things to do than sit in church, like taking a nap, getting dolled up to go out at a nightclub, or just sitting at home. If I was going to be wasting my time doing anything, it certainly wasn't going to be sitting in church. Then I contracted a disease and shortly found out that, *"Hey, this God guy, is pretty legit."* I watched God heal me completely from that disease and I am forever grateful that He didn't hold it against me even when I doubted Him while I was stuck in my own mess. My heart's desire is that everyone could have this type of encounter with God to experience His mercy and radical willingness to forgive us. He is so understanding and compassionate. After God healed me, I vowed to do my best to commit to him and do things the right way because I wanted to be a real Christian, like for real. If I was going to be into this church stuff, I wanted to at least do it right. There were so many Christians who falsely represented God's love; they easily criticized others, and I didn't want to be that way, knowing that I had just been healed from a sexual disease. The trouble that I was in was because of my own wrongdoing, yet God bailed me out, and I didn't want to ruin this newfound relationship. One day in church, I remember thinking "I don't know how to worship God", and I wasn't even sure why I needed to. I had begun to regularly attend church, and during praise and worship I noticed people crying out "I love you, God", and I couldn't fathom how or why there was such an outward expression of worship. For me, this was unnecessary, but as I paid more and more attention to their worship, I began to think "Well, what's wrong with me?" because I surely didn't worship outwardly at all. There was nothing stirring in my heart, at all. I didn't want to be phony or an act-a-liker and worship under pretense. So, I went home after church and began to pray, "Lord, I hear people saying they love you and they worship you openly and outwardly. I don't think I love you yet, but I would like to get to know you and worship you for real. But I can't fake worship, so I won't." I said that prayer and left it right there. I wasn't immediately drawn to outward worship but, eventually, I'd hear a song or two and sing along, then I began to repeat the gospel songs and move to them. Before long, I had my own praise and worship that flowed naturally from my spirit to God. Sometimes we undervalue the principles of worship and what worship really means. I don't believe worship is like the "cha-cha-cha" where everyone can chime in on your personal worship. Worship is a level of intimacy. And I wanted to elevate in my worship to God.

Jesus challenged the woman at the well with her worship. This woman was, in modern day terms, single with a friend. She had a man and they oftentimes Netflix and Chilled! Like Carolyn and my colleagues, she was having a good time and perhaps had gotten used to or acquainted with isolation, she was used to the dirty comments and rumors of her behavior, and the disapproving stares from other women. This Samaritan woman had five husbands, and the man she was currently with wasn't her husband. Perhaps she was still single because she didn't care to be disappointed and heartbroken again, and like many good women who get tired of being mistreated by bad men, she disregarded commitment. Being single may have given her a sense of control because she was finally free from the tyranny of wife duties.

Disappointment causes good women to settle for playing house or being test driven like a car. The Samaritan woman thought it was easier to just move in with the man and not marry. I personally know that it can be difficult to resist the temptation of moving in with a boyfriend (unmarried). One of the first things the devil will tell you is that it would be better to live together than to remain completely single with no one to help with the bills or to bring comfort to you come midnight. But even though this Samaritan woman's exterior appeared shameful, Jesus saw that she was a good woman on the inside, and He knew her willingness to worship, so He challenged her at the well. The reason the Samaritan woman had a life altering encounter with Jesus was because she was real, honest, transparent, and willing to worship. According to Scripture, she was the very first person to whom Jesus announced openly that He was Christ the Messiah. What was it about this outcast, no name, Samaritan woman that caused Jesus to reveal His identity to her? His deity was even hidden to His disciples; the men who followed and served Him. He also hid it from the church folks.

Perhaps, this woman's thirst and hunger for the truth was legitimate and although she may not have been godly, and although her situation was frowned upon, she was what Jesus considered good people.

The word of God says that those who hunger and thirst after righteousness will be filled. He can do miracles in our ordinary lives when we decide to drop our bucket and pale of pride. God rejects the proud but gives grace to the humble. When pride ends, humility starts, and it bridges the gap between grace and goodness. We are all in need of the grace of God because, according to Romans 3:23, "we have all sinned and fallen short of the glory of God." Let us not condemn or stone one another or form cliques to isolate people deemed unfit for acceptance. As we see in the Scriptures, the Samaritan woman was very curious and her intimate conversation with Jesus provided a platform for truthful questions and responses. Value the goodly people and the godly people in your life because God can bless you through them both. Let God be God, and you be willing.

This philosophy has worked for me and I have seen miracles transpire in the lives of so many people by just extending love instead of ridicule. It's love that elevates. Continue in it. Keep climbing. Keep pushing. Remain focused on what lies ahead. Remember that no matter how low life has brought you, leveling up is always possible in Christ. You can elevate without a mate.

About the Author

Vasha Tolbert studied at Bethune Cookman University and Florida Southwestern. She holds her Associates degree in Mass Communications, towards Journalism and Broadcasting. She has also performed a series of radio hosting.

She is the author of *Elevate without a Mate* and is known amongst her peers as an authentic Woman of God, determined, and courageous.

In a world occupied with idolatry and overtaken by immoral explicitness, Vasha delights in impudently advocating the essence of abstinence, equality, and winning while single in Christ. Vasha has mentored and empowered a myriad of singles encouraging others to triumph in the season of singleness.

Connect with Vasha through Social Media.
Website: Vashatolbert.com
Instagram: https://www.instagram.com/vashatolbert/
Facebook: https://elewww.facebook.com/therealvashatolbert or
https://www.facebook.com/vasha.tolbert

CPSIA information can be obtained
at www.ICGtesting.com
Printed in the USA
LVHW110908080521
686863LV00004B/142